MAKING
Chairs & Tables

Volume Two

GUILD OF MASTER CRAFTSMAN PUBLICATIONS LTD

This collection first published 2001 by
Guild of Master Craftsman Publications Ltd
166 High Street, Lewes, East Sussex, BN7 1XU

© GMC Publications Ltd

ISBN 1 86108 275 4

Cover photographs all by Anthony Bailey, except for
front cover, centre right (detail), Stephen Hepworth;
upholstered chairs, centre right, Richard Stephenson

Cover design by Ian Smith, GMC Studio

Colour separation by Viscan Graphics Pte Ltd (Singapore)
Printed and bound by Kyodo Printing (Singapore),
under the supervision of MRM Graphics, Winslow, Bucks, UK

*Note: Every effort has been made to ensure that the information in this book is accurate at the time of
writing but inevitably prices, specifications, and availability of tools will change from time to time. Readers
are therefore urged to contact manufacturers or suppliers for up-to-date information before ordering items.*

CONTENTS

CONVERSION TABLE: MILLIMETRES TO INCHES

mm	inch	mm	inch	mm	inch	mm	inch
1	0.03937	26	1.02362	60	2.36220	310	12.20472
2	0.07874	27	1.06299	70	2.75590	320	12.59842
3	0.11811	28	1.10236	80	3.14960	330	12. 99212
4	0.15748	29	1.14173	90	3.54330	340	13.38582
5	0.19685	30	1.18110	100	3.93700	350	13.77952
6	0.23622	31	1.22047	110	4.33070	360	14.17322
7	0.27559	32	1.25984	120	4.72440	370	14.56692
8	0.31496	33	1.29921	130	5.11811	380	14.96063
9	0.35433	34	1.33858	140	5.51181	390	15.35433
10	0.39370	35	1.37795	150	5.90551	400	15.74803
11	0.43307	36	1.41732	160	6.29921	410	16.14173
12	0.47244	37	1.45669	170	6.69291	420	16.53543
13	0.51181	38	1.49606	180	7.08661	430	16.92913
14	0.55118	39	1.53543	190	7.48031	440	17.32283
15	0.59055	40	1.57480	200	7.87401	450	17.71653
16	0.62992	41	1.61417	210	8.26771	460	18.11023
17	0.66929	42	1.65354	220	8.66141	470	18.50393
18	0.70866	43	1.69291	230	9.05511	480	18.89763
19	0.74803	44	1.73228	240	9.44881	490	19.29133
20	0.78740	45	1.77165	250	9.84252	500	19.68504
21	0.82677	46	1.81102	260	10.23622		
22	0.86614	47	1.85039	270	10.62992		
23	0.90551	48	1.88976	280	11.02362		
24	0.94488	49	1.92913	290	11.41732		
25	0.98425	50	1.96850	300	11.81102		

1 mm = .03937 inch	1 cm = 0.3937 inch	1 m = 3.281 feet
1 inch = 25.4 mm	1 foot = 304.8 mm	1 yard = 914.4 mm

CONVERSION TABLE: INCHES TO MILLIMETRES

inch		mm	inch		mm	inch		mm
1/64	0.01565	0.3969	3/8	0.375	9.5250	47/64	0.734375	18.6531
1/32	0.03125	0.7938	25/64	0.390625	9.9219	3/4	0.750	19.0500
3/64	0.046875	1.1906	13/32	0.40625	10.3188			
1/16	0.0625	1.5875	27/64	0.421875	10.7156	49/64	0.765625	19.4469
						25/32	0.78125	19.8438
5/64	0.078125	1.9844	7/16	0.4375	11.1125	51/64	0.796875	20.2406
3/32	0.09375	2.3812	29/64	0.453125	11.5094	13/16	0.8125	20.6375
7/64	0.109375	2.7781	15/32	0.46875	11.9062			
			31/64	0.484375	12.3031	53/64	0.828125	21.0344
1/8	0.125	3.1750				27/32	0.84375	21.4312
9/64	0.140625	3.5719	1/2	0.500	12.700	55/64	0.858375	21.8281
5/32	0.15625	3.9688	33/64	0.515625	13.0969			
11/64	0.171875	4.3656	17/32	0.53125	13.4938	7/8	0.875	22.2250
			35/64	0.546875	13.8906	57/64	0.890625	22.6219
3/16	0.1875	4.7625	9/16	0.5625	14.2875	29/32	0.90625	23.0188
13/64	0.203125	5.1594				59/64	0.921875	23.4156
7/32	0.21875	5.5562	37/64	0.578125	14.6844			
15/64	0.234375	5.9531	19/32	0.59375	15.0812	15/16	0.9375	23.8125
1/4	0.250	6.3500	39/64	0.609375	15.4781	61/64	0.953125	24.2094
						31/32	0.96875	24.6062
17/64	0.265625	6.7469	5/8	0.625	15.8750	63/64	0.984375	25.0031
9/32	0.28125	7.1438	41/64	0.640625	16.2719			
19/64	0.296875	7.5406	21/32	0.65625	16.6688	1	1.00	25.4
5/16	0.3125	7.9375	43/64	0.671875	17.0656			
21/64	0.1328125	8.3344	11/16	0.6875	17.4625			
11/32	0.34375	8.7312	45/64	0.703125	17.8594			
23/64	0.359375	9.1281	23/32	0.71875	18.2562			

Measurements are in metric with imperial equivalents. Readers should be aware that conversions may have been rounded up or down to the nearest convenient equivalent. Where a measurement is absolute no conversion has been made.

INTRODUCTION

You would perhaps think that there are only so many designs for these very necessary objects. Many might argue that a chair is a seat with four legs and a table has four legs, usually, and a top – and that you can't really improve on this essential theme. This has not stopped furniture-makers from trying. People have been constructing things to sit on and surfaces to perform various tasks on since before Egyptian times, yet makers and designers continually come up with fresh angles. Since its first issue, *Furniture & Cabinetmaking* magazine has featured an array of designs for chairs and tables, but we have merely scratched the surface, metaphorically speaking.

I am constantly inspired and delighted by the different solutions that our talented contributors come up with, which meant making the selection of articles for this volume a difficult task. Not only are their designs different but so too are their methods. Every maker will approach the same problem individually, be it something as basic as cutting a rebate or complex laminating. This individuality of approach is one of the fascinating aspects of woodworking as a whole, not just of furniture-making. All of the approaches and techniques you will find here provide insight into some of the mysteries behind the making process and sometimes afford a glimpse into the thinking behind the ideas.

Tables can represent some of the simplest pieces of furniture to make and offer a good grounding in the one of the oldest joints in woodworking: the mortice and tenon. They can be extremely complex too – once extensions and elliptical tops are introduced. One of the components that can throw up fresh and intriguing designs is the stretcher frame, and you will find some excellent examples in these pages.

Chairs, on the other hand, seem to create a love–hate relationship. Some makers will tackle them only very reluctantly; others relish the challenge. Few chairs have much about them that is a right angle and making a one-off can be far easier than making a set. It is all very well producing a brilliant full-size mock up, but coming up with a design that can be made in multiples is another matter. Many of the most innovative and complex designs in furniture come from chair-making and, to my mind at least, some of the most pleasing derive from the simplest forms.

This collection of projects will help you to decide not only what you do want but what you don't want, too. If any of the designs are not to your personal taste, look instead at the methods the maker has applied: they may offer a solution to another furniture project. Above all, I hope the selection will provide you with stimulating ideas and further enjoyment of the making process.

Colin Eden-Eadon

Colin Eden-Eadon
Editor, *Furniture & Cabinetmaking*

Arthur Cross on making an inexpensive and simple telephone table

PHOTOGRAPHY BY JOHN NEWBERRY

Ringing the changes

MY MODESTLY priced hall/telephone table was born out of the recession. Selling furniture has been difficult during the last few years, and a decline in orders for my more expensive pieces caused a bit of a rethink about what to do next.

There is no shortage of restoration and repolishing, but my heart was not in this work; I also considered making pine furniture which always seems to sell, but felt the market was already saturated.

My table is made in quarter-sawn stainy oak (*Quercus sp*) – variously known according to area as stripy or tiger oak – my favourite timber. Brown oak is caused by a fungal growth; the stripy effect occurs during the development of the fungus, and is an intermediate stage towards brown oak.

The table pictured here is made from a single inexpensive piece of timber – except for the drawer runners and the backs of the drawers which came out

of my stock.

The height of the table should be such so that the client can look up a number from the book without stooping. To make up several, increase the height of the legs; these can always be cut down if required.

The slim legs do require a rail system below, but make sure room is left for the Hoover!

Under bed

This will be the first piece of furniture a visitor will see when he enters the house, so I feel an eye-catching grained piece is important.

For this reason I never use bland timber, although I have made one or two out of pitch pine from a church pew.

I like to bring the timber into the house a month before use, storing it under the bed. I can recall reading about someone sawing up some 300-year-old oak beams only to find these warped all over the place, so released tensions must be allowed for.

Top

In this particular table top and ends the figure of the oak is used to give the impression of telephone messages being transmitted between the two continents.

I have made book-matched tops out of kiln-dried quarter-sawn oak. For this I use timber of around 25mm (1in) thick. I have so far had no problems with movement, but this presents a problem with thicker timber which has not dried out in the centre.

One other way of avoiding some of the problems associated with movement is to do some secondary machining oversize a month or so before taking down to finished dimensions, putting the pieces carefully in stick in between operations.

Machining up in this way will also help with the effects of tension.

Machine up, shoot the edge joints and glue up the boards for the top, then leave to one side to settle down.

● **ARTHUR CROSS has been making furniture just about all his life. His grandfather started the family business in 1890, some seven years before the Gimson and Barnsley workshops were set up, and was influenced by William Morris.**

Table construction

The delicate nature of the
table requires careful attention
to the construction of the legs
and rails, *see fig 1*. The tenons
are deliberately staggered on
the side and back rails to
allow maximum gluing area
without weakening the fine
legs when they are morticed.

The top and bottom front
rails are a bare-faced dovetail
and tenon, with a central stile
tenoned into them, *see fig 2*.
The legs are tapered; the
stretchers are single-tenoned
into the legs; and the top
bearers and blocks are all slot-
screwed — to allow for
shrinkage — and glued.

Drawers

The fronts have been
selected so that the flow of
the grain goes across the
front for effect; the sides and
back and the bottom are
6mm (¹⁄₄in) thick
approximately, and
dovetailed in the usual way.

Drawer slips are used to allow
for the thinner drawer side this
piece demands. Any traditional
style is suitable.

The bottom extends beyond
the back 3mm (¹⁄₈in) to allow
for any slight shrinkage. The
handles on my table are shaped
like telephones, but the choice
is the maker's.

Assembly is fairly

BELOW LEFT:
Fig 1, showing
staggered tenons
on back and side
rails

BELOW RIGHT: Fig
2, showing side
and front
construction

straightforward. Make sure the
unit is standing square before
fitting the drawer runners and
kickers — always an awkward
procedure.

Line these up using a spirit
level cramped in position.
When the glue has dried fit
screws. This device may
also be used instead of winding
sticks to save all that bending
down!

Finish

I use Rustins' grain filler followed
by several applications of Jaxalac
Satin Lacquer No. 90/492A, with
hardener B, supplied by
Sonneborn & Rieck Ltd of
Hainault, Essex. This is available
only in five litre containers. I use
it slightly thinned down, applying
it with a french polisher's rubber.
The company's stain can also be
used with this lacquer.

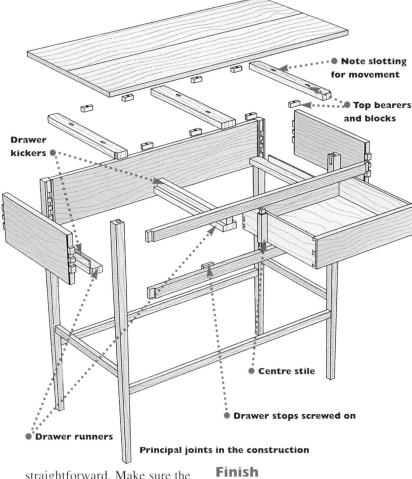

Note slotting
for movement

Top bearers
and blocks

Drawer
kickers

Centre stile

Drawer stops screwed on

Drawer runners

Principal joints in the construction

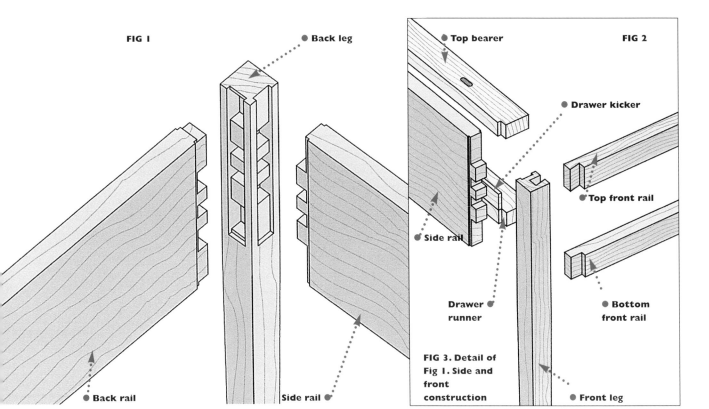

FIG 1

Back leg

Top bearer

FIG 2

Drawer kicker

Side rail

Top front rail

Back rail

Side rail

Drawer
runner

FIG 3. Detail of
Fig 1. Side and
front
construction

Bottom
front rail

Front leg

Simply geometric

David Gregson makes a curvaceous expanding table

MAIN ILLUSTRATION BY IAN HALL

● **DAVID GREGSON is a self-taught cabinetmaker who has been making and taking commissions for the last 20 years. His work is defined by simple geometry and his love of curves.**

BELOW: Fine curves echoed throughout make an elegant dining set

THE DESIGNS for this suite of dining furniture started when the clients saw one of my dining tables with double arched underframing. This particular table had the arches springing from the bottom of the legs, but they expressed a desire to have a lighter feel to the table and for the flowing lines of the underframing to be continued in chairs, a sideboard, a mirror and a low table. The theme of lightness was to be continued in the choice of maple (*Acer saccharum*) for the whole suite.

Design

I decided to spring the arches from a point about one third of the way up the legs which gives a visual lightness without sacrificing any of the strength of the structure; and to enhance this, turned tapered legs and sculptured joints were decided on. To soften the edges and to continue the theme of flowing lines, the ends of the top were curved with radiused corners and the edge was

> "I decided to spring the arches from a point about one third of the way up the legs which gives a visual lightness without sacrificing any of the strength of the structure"

given a semi-circular cross section.

The table was designed to seat six, with an extension leaf dropped in the middle to accommodate ten: the dimensions being 2100 by 1070mm (6ft 10¹¹⁄₁₆in by 3ft 6⅛in) extending to 2700mm (8ft 10⅝in)

Leaves

The tops and extension leaves are traditionally jointed using sprung joints. You can either make them up first and leave them to settle while the undercarriage structure is built, which will allow you to adjust any movement that might occur before fitting and finishing – or sometimes it is better to make them up once the main frame is finished, fit them to the running carriage, and finish them, hoping that this will retard any movement. Either way, be aware of the variables of the climate and don't do things like leave the tops in front of a sunny window with the edges exposed!

Construction

The construction is essentially four triangular assemblies, each consisting of a leg, a top rail and half an arch. Complicated constructions always need full size drawings to work out precisely how the joints should be made, the exact relationship of the various components and, in curved and sculptured work, the exact arc of the curves and the amount of wood needed for the sculptured joints.

As all the legs are turned, the rails have to be sculptured into them both on their two faces and on the top and bottom surfaces.

Legs, mortices and tenons

All the main leg joints are morticed and tenoned. This includes the curved end rails, diagonal rails, and where the laminated arch meets the leg. The mortices are cut in the legs while they are still blanks, and as much waste is removed as possible with the bandsaw leaving the blocks for the sculptured joints sticking out. The legs can then be turned, taking care to avoid contact with the blocks!

There is a curved end rail between the tops of the legs at each end, the main part of which is jointed to the legs with mortice and tenons, the top part being the end of the framework of the extension mechanism. I used one piece of oversize wood for each of these end rails so that the grain matches, cutting the tenons first, then shaping the curved faces and finally cutting off the top part for later joining to the extension runners. By this method the curve of each part lines up perfectly.

> "The construction is essentially four triangular assemblies, each consisting of a leg, a top rail and half an arch"

ABOVE: Sideboard and mirror subtly complement table and chairs

BELOW: With extension in the table, ten people can be seated

Arches

The arches are laminated half an arch at a time, using 103mm (⅛in) laminates per arch – then blocks are glued to both ends to make up the top of the sculptured joint to the leg, and for the joint to the top rail, *see fig 1*. The tenons are then cut on the end of the arches and inserted into the legs to mark the profile of the arched rail on the leg. The waste on the leg can now be removed to this line, using a carving gouge for the concave areas, and a block plane for the convex faces, sanding to a smoothly flowing joint after assembly.

Outside rails

The two long side rails on the outside of the top rails have an un-glued mortice and tenon joint cut at an angle into the side of each triangular assembly. The un-glued joint is to enable the table to be dis-assembled. The dry joint is held in place by screws. The two rails also act as guides for the extension frames and join exactly at the point where the diagonal rails have their cut-out, *see fig 2*.

BELOW: Fig 1 Structure of the leg arches

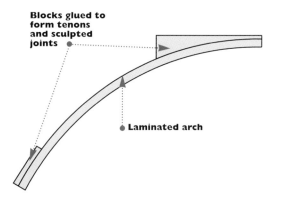

Blocks glued to form tenons and sculpted joints

Laminated arch

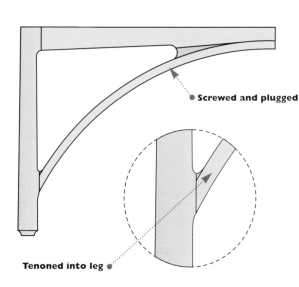

Screwed and plugged

Tenoned into leg

Construction

Machine four top rails, cut the tenons and the profile and cut out the area where the sliding runner frame will go.

At this point the angled mortices for the long outside rails, that act as guides, need to be cut – it is much easier to do this now rather than later when the frames are glued-up. It will need careful dry-cramping to test fit everything – this is where a good setting out or full drawing is worth its weight in gold!

Flat faces are worked on the inside of the areas where the tops of the arches meet the top rail so that they can be glued, screwed and plugged together. The four assemblies each consisting of one leg, one laminated arch, and one top rail are now put together.

> "The two long side rails on the outside of the top rails have an un-glued mortice and tenon joint cut at an angle into the side of each triangular assembly"

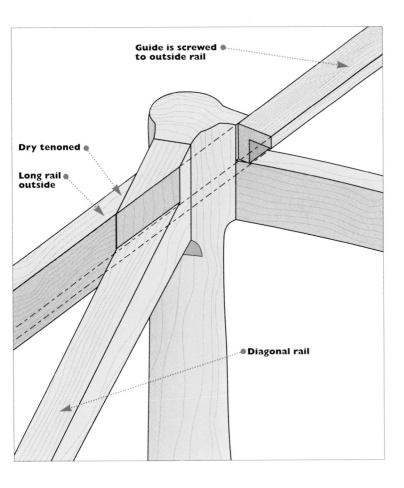

Guide is screwed to outside rail

Dry tenoned

Long rail outside

Diagonal rail

"The two rails also act as guides for the extension frames and join exactly at the point where the diagonal rails have their cut-out"

LEFT: Fig 2 How the two types of leg rail meet and help to act as guides.

BELOW: The laminated arches provide strength without stretcher rails getting in the way

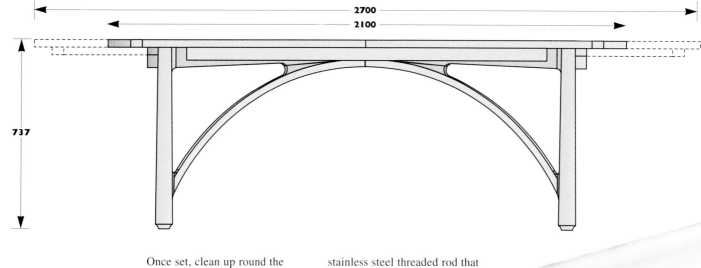

2700
2100
737

Once set, clean up round the sculpted joints and shape the un-turned areas of legs to a circular profile.

Join pairs of these assemblies with the curved end rails between the tops of the legs; the area where the top rail/arches meet is cut at an angle so that it can be screwed, glued and plugged.

Stainless steel rod

There are now two assemblies each consisting of: two legs, two arches, two top rails, and an end rail. These are held together by a stainless steel threaded rod that passes through triangular blocks. The blocks are needed to give a flat face on which to tighten a dome headed hexagon nut at each end which pulls the tops of the arches tightly together. Glue the triangular blocks into the acute angle where the top rails/arches meet on each assembly.

A cross rail is half-lapped, again dry, and held with screws across the middle of the table through the two assembled ends, and half-lapped into the long side rails, *see main drawing.*

Guides and runners

Make up four rebated lengths of oak, to act as guides, and screw two of them to the top of the inside faces of the two long side rails with their rebates downwards.

Make up two oak frames from the other two rebated pieces, which will be the runners, joined by three cross rails, so that they can slide between the guides, *see main drawing*.

The pieces of maple that were cut from the curved end rails earlier are now stub-tenoned to the outer end of each runner frame, so that it is flush with the rest of the curved end rail when the centre end of

the runner frame meets the cross rail in the centre.

The whole runner frame assembly is now screwed to the undersides of the end leaves; drill holes in the centre line of the table and slot screw holes on either side to allow for movement.

Finish

The table is finished with three coats of a pre-catalyst matt lacquer, sanded and de-nibbed between coats.

In the following article David Gregson makes the chairs to match his table.

"The two end table leaves locate together, one with a tongue and the other with a groove where they meet"

Chairs to match

In the second of his two-part project **David Gregson** makes the chairs to go with his extending table

● **DAVID GREGSON** is a self-taught cabinetmaker who has been making and taking commissions for the last 20 years. His work is defined by simple geometry and his love of curves.

L EADING ON from the previous project in which I made an extending dining table in maple (*Acer saccharum*), it is time to turn to the matching chairs – which proved not to be as simple as they seemed!

Legs

The curved and turned back legs of the chairs can be made in two ways: you could bandsaw them out of the solid and shape them by hand – but this seems like a lot of work because of the fact that the circular cross section, and the blocks that have to be left for the sculptured joints, get in the way. Alternatively they can be turned, and then steam bent to the curve.

I decided to take the latter option, so, once the commission was confirmed, and six months before starting work on the chairs, I decided to try steam bending. A test leg which was turned and had the blocks for the joints left on, but without the mortices cut, bent perfectly – and I looked forward to making the chairs having, I thought, resolved the main process by which the back legs were to be made.

The turning of the legs is done by wedging the blocks for the side seat rail joints into a 63mm (2½in) internal diameter, bearing-mounted on the lathe to prevent whipping.

ABOVE: Back of carver showing laminated slots and bottom back rail

STEAM BENDING

A simple steam bending system can be made by using a standard 200mm (8in) plastic soil pipe and a steam wallpaper stripper. The pipe can be bought with threaded ends and screw-on caps. You will need to make a ladder-like structure to go inside to act as a platform for your wood to sit on. A hole is drilled in the side of the soil pipe to take the pipe of the stripper – a plastic threaded pipe-connector will act as a seal between them. 12mm (½in) wood will probably need about half an hour. For bending thicker material you will need a more substantial steam box and more time.

ABOVE: The theme of sculptured joints and turned legs is continued in the chairs

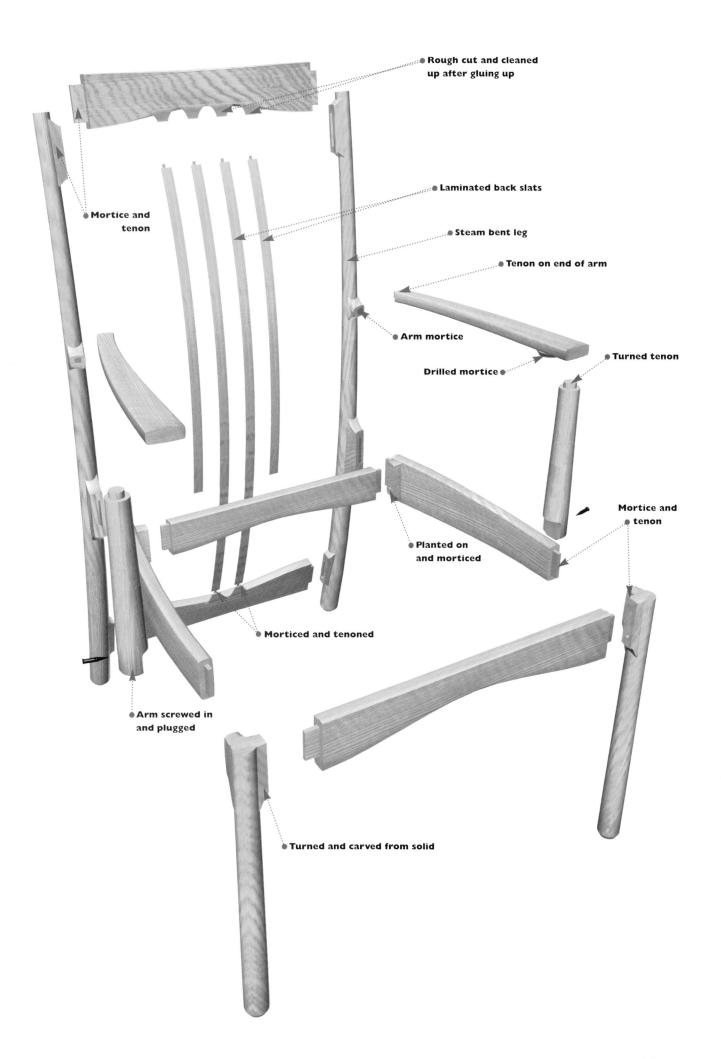

Rough cut and cleaned up after gluing up

Mortice and tenon

Laminated back slats

Steam bent leg

Tenon on end of arm

Arm mortice

Drilled mortice

Turned tenon

Planted on and morticed

Mortice and tenon

Morticed and tenoned

Arm screwed in and plugged

Turned and carved from solid

"Once the commission was confirmed, and six months before starting work on the chairs, I decided to try steam bending"

Problems

The next job was the steam bending. The first pair of legs that I examined on removal from the formers showed some cracking around the side seat rail joint blocks – both on the end grain areas that I had bandsawn to shape above and below the joint, and on the sides of the joint faces. I tried a few more of my carefully turned and pre-morticed legs, and ended up with about 60% of them having cracks in this area. The rest of the leg was fine.

"I looked forward to making the chairs having, I thought, resolved the main process by which the back legs were to be made"

I decided that even though I had used shaped blocks to hold these areas down in the formers, the difference in thickness at this point, and the short grain due to the pre-cut mortices, were always going to cause problems. It was also possible that the wood, having been stored in the workshop for six months, was just that bit too dry.

"I tried a few more of my carefully turned and pre-morticed legs, and ended up with about 60% of them having cracks in this area"

Solutions

Rather than try to cut the legs out of the solid with new wood, which I would have had to condition for several weeks at least, I consulted with my clients at this point and suggested that I could cut out these defective areas and, by carefully selecting wood to match the grain, glue in pieces to replace them.

Again I did a trial and, having shown my clients, I proceeded with the work of gluing these pieces in and re-morticing, which required carefully mounting in the morticer as the legs were now turned, tapered and curved.

Back slats

The back slats are laminated from three 3.3mm (⅛in) pieces and their back faces profiled to a semi-circle on a router table. Because they are only 10mm (⅜in) thick and are sculptured into the top and bottom rails, their tenons have to be very small – I used my router with a 5mm (³⁄₁₆in) long cutter to form the mortices.

Assembly

Although much of the waste can be removed from the sculptured areas before assembly, most of the work in these joints has to be done after gluing-up. To facilitate this, glue-up the back legs with their top and bottom rails, and the two centre slats, and then shape all these joints before gluing the back leg assembly to the rest of the chair parts and the two side slats.

ABOVE: **Arched front seat rail reflects the shape of the top back rail**

BELOW: **Side profile of carver**

FURTHER INFORMATION

David Colwell's excellent video *Bending Solid Timber*, GMC £15.21 inc VAT is a mine of information on how this renowned designer of steam bent furniture goes about it.
ISBN 1 86108 081 6

Fine Woodworking on Bending Wood has masses of good advice on steam bending and laminating.
Taunton Press £8.95 ISBN 0 918804 29 9

Made to exhibit

A hall table in maple and Santos rosewood by **Richard Jones**

THIS HALL TABLE in maple (*Acer spp*) and Santos rosewood (*Dalbergia nigra*) is one of my range of exhibition pieces. It came about through an idea I had for a tall and elegant table whose location might be a large hallway or reception area of a house, hotel or business.

Design
In the early sketching stages I decided on three design elements – a version of the cabriole leg would be used; the top would float above the supporting framework; and a light coloured timber for the leg structure would be contrasted with a dark top.

Curves in the leg suggested the detailing of smaller and complementary features throughout the piece – the front of the table top, and front rail and stretcher curve, were to reflect the leg's long sweep.

The rear broken architectural-style upstand is pierced centrally, and curved at both ends to mirror the top of the leg, and the front and side edges of the top are bevelled at a low angle to show a slim edge.

The front and back rail are slightly narrower than the thickness of the leg top to create a small offset in the mortice and tenon joint. Intermediate cross-rails to carry the top are stopped-dovetail-housed to the inner faces of the front and back rails, and protrude above them by 25mm (1in). Stretchers provide additional strength.

I had a couple of slight variations in mind for the form of the stretchers, to be decided as I went along.

Working drawing
I normally do a working drawing to eliminate time-consuming design work in the workshop, but on this occasion details were unresolved. It can be rewarding and exciting to solve these as the piece comes together.

Hard maple is used for the under-framing, and a trip to the local timber yard yielded some Santos rosewood that suited.

The full size and shape of the cabriole leg is laid out, marking the vertical positions of the mortices on an MDF template. This is cut to shape and cleaned up. A common fault with cabriole legs is to make the curves pronounced, thereby creating two problems – it gives them a deformed and bandy appearance and can cause weaknesses due to short grain. To overcome both these shortcomings it

● **RICHARD JONES** trained as a cabinetmaker and, after some years as a craftsman with furniture workshops, spent nine years teaching MA students of Furniture Design & Craft at Heriot Watt University in Edinburgh. He specialises in the design and production of fine contemporary pieces as well as antique restoration, and is now settled in the USA

> "The rear broken architectural-style upstand is pierced centrally, and curved at both ends to mirror the top of the leg"

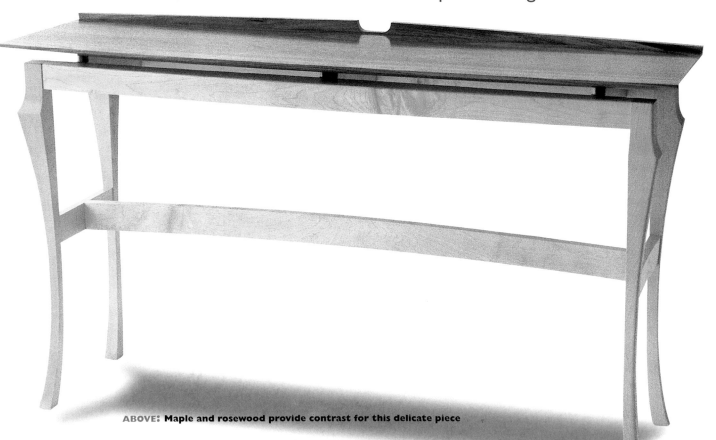

ABOVE: Maple and rosewood provide contrast for this delicate piece

is essential to ensure that at least a 4
to 6mm (⁵⁄₃₂ to ¼in) square section of
timber runs right through the leg
from top to bottom – this also helps
by forcing the designer to lay out a
graceful form!

Construction

All the materials are machined up
first from a cutting list.

Three rosewood planks were
selected for the top, with curved
grain in the front plank picked to
closely match the planned curvature
of the front. These are edged,
followed by a couple of skims with
a try-plane to form a minuscule
spring – biscuit joints are cut to help
alignment. The plank formed is
machine-surfaced and thicknessed,
then left to settle during under-frame
construction. Biscuits can telegraph
through to polished surfaces if
insufficient time is left between
glue-up and finishing.

Legs and rails

The legs were selected so that the
grain followed the curvature in the
cabriole form. Each leg was
allocated a corner so as to optimise
the most attractive grain at the
front. An extra leg was cut out of
poplar (*Liriodendron tulipifera*)
for experimentation. The template
was used to trace the shape on the
two inner faces of each leg,
transferring the mortice marks to
the relevant faces.

The rails are machined 350mm
(14in) over-length to make practice
tenons. The figure of the front rail
was quarter-sawn, that is straight-
grained, which wasn't decorative
enough. A 3 to 4mm (⅛in) piece of
through-sawn timber will be glued
to the front face later.

All the under-frame joints are laid
out and cut, using the practice
pieces for accuracy. For example,
two extra-long mortices are worked
in the sample poplar leg, so that the
twin sloping haunched tenons on the
rails can be test-fitted to it. The offcut from the rails is used to set up
the tenons.

Rail dovetails

The dovetails and housings are
routed. A dovetail cutter is fixed in
the router and set to 10mm (⅜in)
deep. A straight-edge is used to
determine the offset of the cutter
from the edge of the router base in a
piece of scrap. Once this is
established, the straight-edge is
clamped to the inner faces of the
rails, this distance from the required
position for the dovetail housing.
Each cut is started from the top of

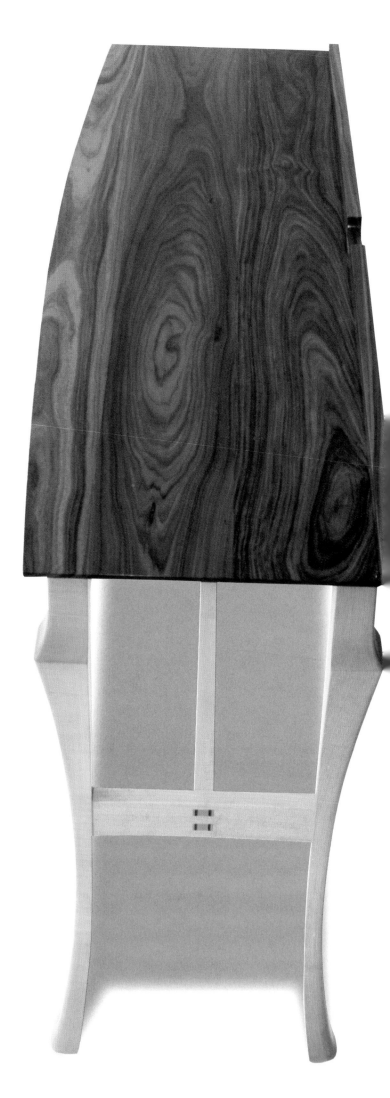

the rail, and stopped short of the bottom of the rail by some 13mm (½in). The end of the housing is squared out with chisels to 10mm (⅜in) short of the bottom edge.

Next, the cutter and router are mounted in a table, and the three rails individually attached to a vertical jig. The depth and width of cut required is set by trial and error. The dovetails are cut in two passes, one either side. The shoulders to match the 10mm (⅜in) stopped-end of the housing on the long rails are cut on the table-saw using the sliding table. The chamfers on the top of the joint are formed on the saw as the last operation. The rails are then drilled to screw the top down.

"The long curved stretcher is drawn by using the two pins and stick method"

Stretchers and front rail

The long curved stretcher is drawn by using the two pins and stick method again, followed by bandsawing and spokeshaving. It is joined to the short stretchers with wedged mortice and tenons. It is time-consuming and pernickety, but decorative and strong!

The inside face of the short stretchers is flat. The outside has compound curves and tapers to follow the leg shape. These are marked free-hand, cut on the bandsaw, and fine-tuned by the compass plane and spokeshave again. These short stretchers are joined to the leg with a standard mortice and tenon.

The curve of the front rail is laid out using two pins nailed to thin plywood, and springing a slender stick between them. The plywood is cut to form a template and offered to the top edge of the front rail for tracing. The rail is bandsawn and cleaned up, preparing a surface for the veneer.

The veneer face of the rail is made by squaring and thickness-planing a thick piece of stock from which a 5mm (³⁄₁₆in) off-cut is sawn on the table-saw. The sawn face of the thick piece is then re-thicknessed, and the second 5mm (³⁄₁₆in) off-cut ripped off by re-setting the saw fence. The two pieces produced are thicknessed to about 3mm (⅛in).

ABOVE: Graceful shape of leg is taken from the traditional shape of the cabriole

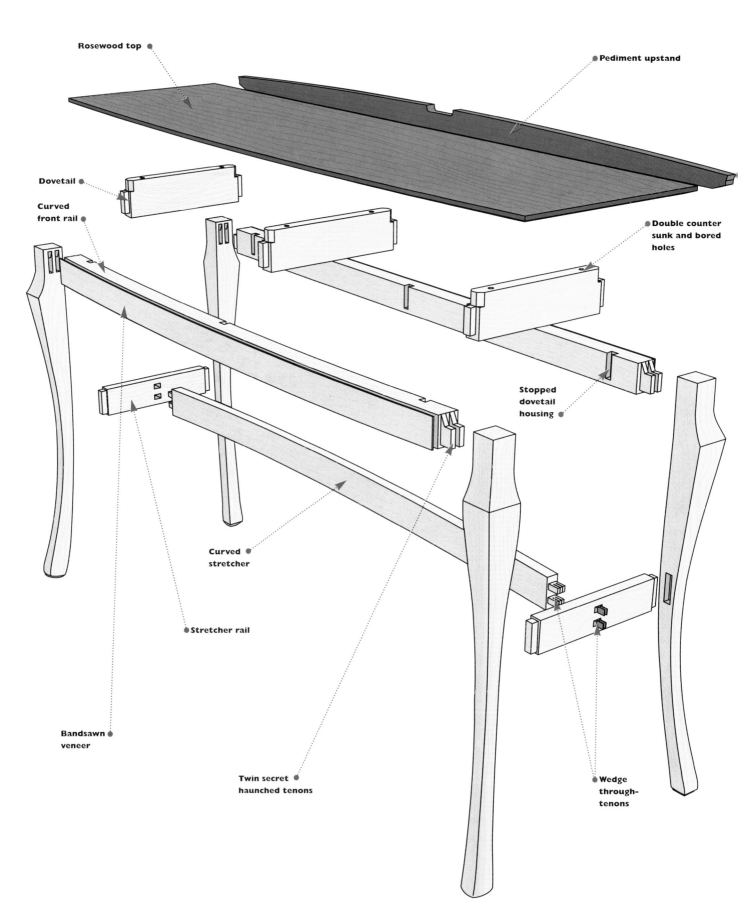

Rosewood top

Pediment upstand

Dovetail

Curved front rail

Double counter sunk and bored holes

Stopped dovetail housing

Curved stretcher

Stretcher rail

Bandsawn veneer

Twin secret haunched tenons

Wedge through-tenons

"The small broken-arched pediment-style upstand at the back is biscuited on after the central curved cut-out and curved ends are formed"

These pieces are glued into place using 6mm (¼in) MDF to spread the cramping pressure – polyurethane glue is used for this because it has a long open time. After cleaning-up and squeezing the glue out, the shoulder lines on the tenons are re-defined, and a bevel worked on the top front rail edges so that it runs out right on the glue line. This disguises the join and any changes in grain pattern.

The legs are bandsawn to shape, followed by a compass-plane, spokeshaves, stationary belt sander, scrapers, and abrasive papers to refine the shape and round-over the sharp front edges and foot. I made comparisons from one leg to the other as I went along.

Assembly

Prior to assembly, all parts that can be, are sanded to 220 grit abrasive. The structure is assembled in four stages – firstly, join the long stretcher to the two short stretchers, and drive the wedges in. After drying, the wedges are cleaned flush to the curved shape of the short stretchers.

Next, the legs are glued to the long rails, followed by the H-shaped stretcher parts being glued into their lower leg mortices.

Then the sliding dovetails on the intermediate rails are glued into place by sliding each one down individually, thus revealing one reason for selecting this joint in the first place – it allowed a much less stressful gluing-up procedure! After each stage of the glue-up, complete any trimming and sanding necessary.

Top curve

With the under-frame complete, the table top can be finished. I checked mine for distortion and found it had moved only a little during storage. Minor flattening was

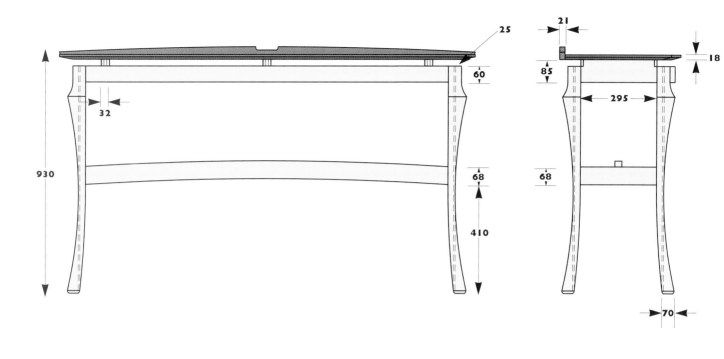

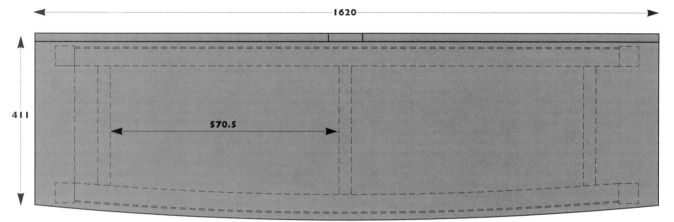

"I made comparisons from one leg to the other as I went along"

done on the surface-planer and then it was thickness-planed. The whole was then squared-up by truing the back edge of the top on the surface-planer, and cut to size on the panel saw.

The front curve is traced from the plywood template made earlier, jigsawn and smoothed. The bevel on the underside is roughed-out in stages with a router, side-fence and straight-cutter, and finished with hand-planes. This rosewood had a lot of interlocked and twisted grain, so the top and bottom were sanded in increments from 120 grit to 220 grit on a panel sander, thereby saving a lot of hand-planing and scraping. Hand-

sanding completed the process to 320 grit.

The small broken-arched pediment-style upstand at the back is biscuited on after the central curved cut-out and curved ends are formed. The top is fitted to the under-frame, and removed again for polishing.

Finishing

The under-frame is finished with five coats of tung oil. It is fairly easy to damage, but simple to repair, has a nice feel to the touch, and darkens maple satisfactorily.

All faces of the top are sprayed with three coats of satin pre-catalysed lacquer, rubbing down nibs in between. The top coat is finished with 0000 wire wool and liquid wax. Pre-catalysed lacquer was chosen for its ability to resist liquid and other damage. Should there be a need to re-finish in the future, the top can easily be removed.

"Should there be a need to re-finish in the future, the top can easily be removed"

LEFT: Beveled underneath of top helps lighten the visual impression while keeping a sensible thickness

Full support

PHOTOGRAPHY BY LEE SIMPSON

● **MICHAEL NORRIS** trained as an architect, going on to practise as an architectural model-maker. He had no formal training in wood-working. Before his untimely death, he taught Spatial Design and Product Design at Kent Institute of Art and Design in Rochester.

Michael Norris makes a chair that combines support with elegance

FOR A LONG TIME I have been striving to find a chair design that integrates angles that are good for human posture support, with angles that create an elegant and wise chair structure.

Dimensions
The chair's structure has to be manoeuvred and cajoled so as not to impede or intrude on the sitter, rather than the other way round! My starting point has always been the angles and their relevant positions to each other.

The seat needs to be 450mm (17¾in) off the floor, with a slope down at 4° from horizontal, front to back. The back support needs to slope back and up at an angle of 15° from vertical, with its lowest extent 200mm (8in) above the seat and 50mm (2in) back from the seat.

The most important area to leave free of structure is the space below the back support and the seat – if the sitter's bottom can't protrude beyond the back of the seat, the small of the back cannot reach the back support.

Chair I & II
The initial intention for Chair I was to try and simplify the seat and frame used in earlier designs. I gave it a mix of webbing from front to back, interwoven with hardwood slats from side to side – allowing for a degree of 'give', and a secondary cradling effect, without the sitter touching the frame. The seat and back frame were reduced to just two beams – a total of four beams joining and spanning the two leg structures.

ABOVE: Triangles in construction lend rigidity

Chair II has a triangulated frame off the back legs, using mortices, tenons, and wedged pegs.

The method by which the beams are integrated with the chair structure is the most important discovery I have made in over twenty years of chair designing – certainly for chairs with frames.

Structure
The cross beams forming the two leg structures are jointed in two very distinct ways depending on the particular dual roles each is playing, both in terms of posture support and structure of chair.

Looking at the chairs from the side, the front cross beam is in line with the cantilever, so they join with a mortice and tenon. The back beam, however, is lifted out of line – it is offset, and rests on top of the cantilever.

> "The chair's structure has to be manoeuvred and cajoled so as not to impede or intrude on the sitter"

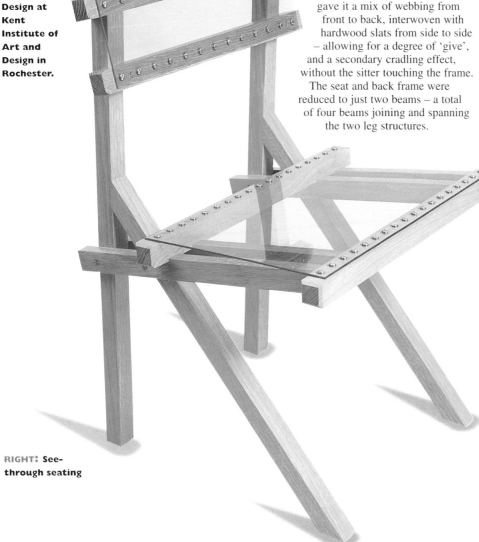

RIGHT: See-through seating

The cantilever is allowed to pass the beam unaltered, apart from a small angled rebate to form a single shoulder. In addition, a peg holds the two members together ensuring the effectiveness of the shoulder – this shoulder is important to resist movement under tension from webbing, sheet ply or plastic.

Breakthrough

It was while drawing Chair I that the full significance of this 'offset' came to light. It was enough that there was space below and in front of the back cross beam – a natural space for deflection of webs and slats, but it was also significant that the back beam or stretcher does not have to weaken the cantilever. The back support structure was kept away from obstructing the sitter's bottom, with no real need for a double crank – the advantages seemed endless!

It was in fact during my attempts to eliminate this crank behind the back support that the breakthrough occurred. I noticed that if the back support structure was brought nearer to vertical, and if the top of the back support were lowered, then the offset allowed both correct back support at 15° one side of vertical, and back support structure at 9° the other side of vertical. This 3° made a perfect line, not only for back support structure but also for the back leg – the two could become one.

At the same time the seat offset was providing an exaggerated amount of space for the sitter's bottom, and some of this could be used to widen the angle for the front leg, which could be raised.

After what seemed like a lifetime of trying to create a structural triangle behind the seat, there it was, well out of the way of backs and bottoms, while providing stability both from front to back, and indirectly from side to side.

Refinements

A small concession to the need for strength meant that the two cantilevers should be recessed each by 2 to 5mm (⅛ to ¼in) into the leg – the resulting double shoulder for each cantilever meant that the peg

and glue in this joint would not take all the strain.

A further refinement made sure that there will be only the lower shoulder and chamfer, 2.5mm (⅛in) deep, which will house the inner bevelled side of each of the paired cantilevers. This is an efficient, and almost foolproof, configuration which matches the chamfer and single shoulder used for joining offset beam to cantilever. Both joints, of course, still rely on the faithful old wedged peg to hold them together.

Simplicity

To complete the simplicity of this chair I decided to use 3mm (⅛in) thick plastic sheet on the seat and the back. The sheets are held in place with stainless steel screws, and do not totally cover the beams – about 15mm (⅝in) of beam will show at each end and 2.5mm (⅛in) at front and back, showing where the support for the seat and back surface is coming from.

Plastic

The plastic is Darvic, which is an extremely versatile material with a hard surface and is capable of being moulded, although it also has 'memory' and can be restored to its original flat state.

I discovered that the makers of Darvic plastic now produce a beautiful clear tinted sheet which is surface hardened and high impact-proof. The result is stunning, and has made a chair that is 'there but not there'. The two surfaces are shiny and 'twinkle', and are enhanced by the stainless steel fixings. It is great to see the chair's structure through the seat and the back – even the wedged pegs holding the offset frames are now visible. Darvic is also a joy to use – it circular saws cleanly with the blade low, and with no chipping, and it planes smoothly by machine or by hand – it even scrapes extremely well when small bevels are needed on exposed sharp edges.

"It is great to see the chair's structure through the seat and the back"

ABOVE: Note double seat rails notched into back legs

BELOW: Opaque seat material for the more modest

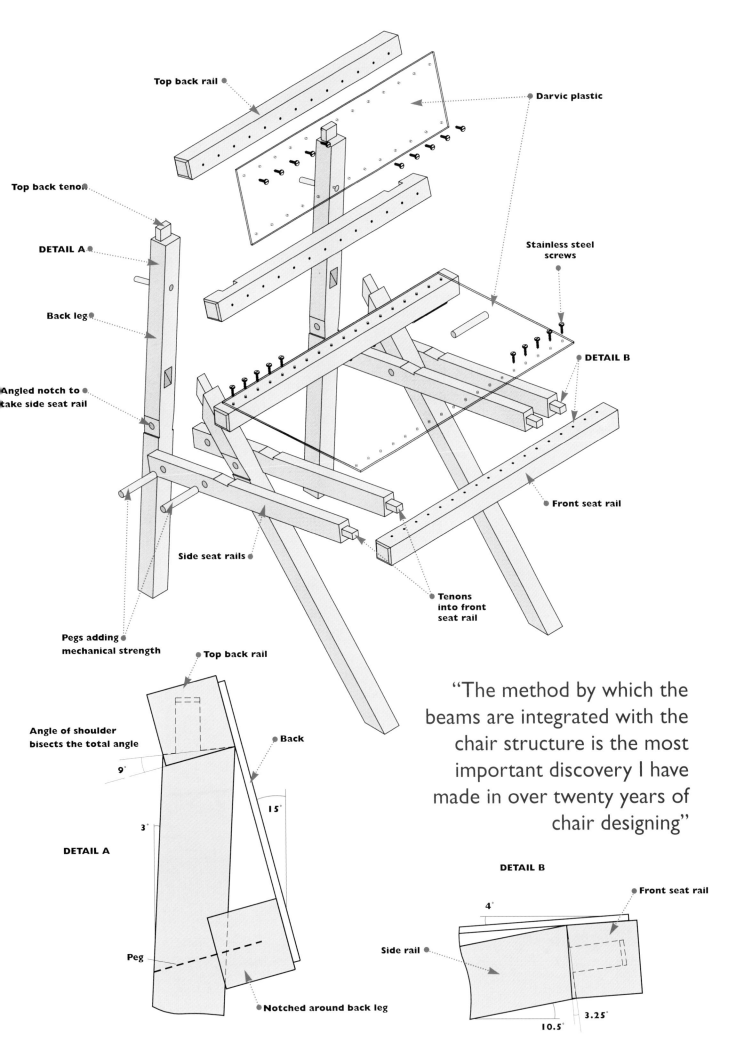

Top back rail

Darvic plastic

Top back tenon

DETAIL A

Stainless steel screws

Back leg

DETAIL B

Angled notch to take side seat rail

Front seat rail

Side seat rails

Tenons into front seat rail

Pegs adding mechanical strength

Top back rail

Angle of shoulder bisects the total angle

Back

9°

15°

3°

DETAIL A

Peg

Notched around back leg

"The method by which the beams are integrated with the chair structure is the most important discovery I have made in over twenty years of chair designing"

DETAIL B

Front seat rail

4°

Side rail

3.25°

10.5°

Perfect pair

Mike Cowie makes
matching side tables

PHOTOGRAPHY BY STEPHEN HEPWORTH
ILLUSTRATION BY IAN HALL AND SIMON RODWAY

Mike Cowie turned to cabinetmaking after
being made redundant five years ago. He
took a City & Guilds course at Sheffield
College which he passed with distinction,
set up his own workshop, and is now in the
happy position of having as much work as
he can cope with

Clean lines and understated detail are the essence of these side tables

I have made several types of these side tables over the last few years, and they have proved to be quite popular. The pair featured here have an Arts & Crafts feel, and are constructed from wych elm *(Ulmus spp)* with two drawers.

I always make the tables in pairs which is more efficient than making them singly, and keeps the price realistic.

"I always make the tables in pairs which is more efficient than making them singly, and keeps the price realistic"

Preparation

The basic carcass is formed from 44 by 20mm (1¾ by ¾in) stock.

Cut and plane the wood for the carcass, then stack it together in an open pile, weighed down, allowing the air to circulate.

The intervening time can be used to prepare the rest of the materials – all the solid wood, top side and back panels. These need to be selected, planed to thickness, and jointed where necessary.

The elements of the drawers can also join the waiting stack to allow them to air before dovetailing.

Carcass construction

Construction of the carcass begins with ensuring that all the pieces are cut to length with square ends – for this, a cut-off box on the table-saw turns a chore into an easy task, *see sidebar*.

Mortices are marked and chopped out with the aid of the router, squaring up the ends with a chisel.

For the tenons, again use the table-saw, although this time with a tenoning jig, which can also be used to cut the bridle joint used on the bottom of the legs.

The back panel is solid and grooved into the rails

A small element of inlay is introduced into the top

Stretcher rail detail

Elm

Elm is a wonderful wood which has a depth that is unmatched by other woods, and is particularly suited to an oil finish. However, my first experience of elm was during my City and Guilds furniture-making course at Sheffield College – I was making a small coffer and had a nice board of elm cut to size and planed to finished dimensions, which I left overnight so that I could joint it the next day. The following morning my elm was so twisted and bent that I binned it and made the coffer in oak.

So it was with caution that I returned to elm – liking the wood but not its tendency to tear-out and distort – although this is the reason for its beauty, its wild grain. The only answer is sharp tools, careful selection, and fast work!

Elm sold through the wood-yard is usually of all the species mixed together and it is pot luck what you get. Dutch elm disease is having a great impact now with little quality material available and American imported elm becoming the norm.

Finishing tenons

At this point I give a finishing touch to my tenons as they tend to be a little ragged, straight from the saw – I cut them slightly oversize, then lay two of the work-pieces down, with the tenon end perpendicular, so that both pieces can be bridged by the router base. I set the router with a dovetail cutter adjusted to trim the tenon, and I check the fit and alter it until it is perfect – this is almost as good as a tenoner, although care must be taken with the procedure because the work-piece is held in the left hand while routing with the right.

I use this method for the sake of speed – for the occasional use it is a simple matter to construct a jig that allows the router to be used with more safety in mind and achieve the same results. Incidentally, a dovetail cutter is used to allow a full cut into the edge without nibbling the shoulder.

Fitting

Make double through-tenons with padauk *(Pterocarpus spp)* wedges at the top and middle, front and back. The sides are jointed with blind tenons and bridle joints on the bottoms. The upper drawer rails are tenoned into the legs with the runners stub-tenoned into the rails.

Do a dry assembly to check for accuracy, and at the same time decide which is to be the front, so that the sides and back can be marked for grooving to accept the panels. The grooves are cut with a 4mm (⅙in) cutter in the router.

The panels can now be cut to size allowing 2mm (⅙in) for movement and the edges shaped with a half round cutter, the back then trimmed with a rebate until a snug fit is achieved in the grooves.

Glue-up

The panels are cleaned up and polished before insertion to prevent lines showing should they shrink.

Glue up the sides first, remembering the panels – a favourite trick of mine!

Ensure that everything is square, and when dry, the remaining rails can be added, using clamps while the wedges

The drawer fronts are cut from a single board giving a matched pair. The top drawer has a lip to cover the drawer rail which allows this to be used to best effect. Handles are rough cut on the bandsaw and cleaned up with a router jig. Cedar of Lebanon drawer bottoms add a finishing touch.

Tenons are cut using a table-saw and cleaned up using a router with the base bridging across the rails with a dovetail cutter to allow a full cut without damaging the shoulders. Mortices are cut with the router as well. Double through-tenons are used on the top and middle, front and back. The sides have blind tenons into the legs. The legs have bridle joints and another through-tenon on the stretcher rail keeps them from splaying.

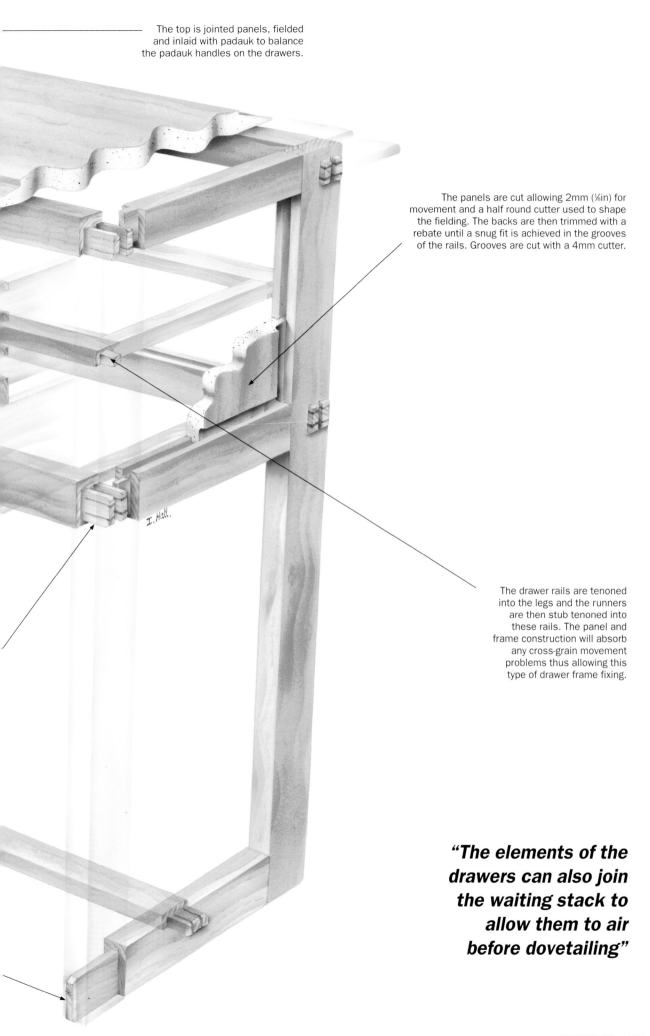

The top is jointed panels, fielded and inlaid with padauk to balance the padauk handles on the drawers.

The panels are cut allowing 2mm (⅛in) for movement and a half round cutter used to shape the fielding. The backs are then trimmed with a rebate until a snug fit is achieved in the grooves of the rails. Grooves are cut with a 4mm cutter.

The drawer rails are tenoned into the legs and the runners are then stub tenoned into these rails. The panel and frame construction will absorb any cross-grain movement problems thus allowing this type of drawer frame fixing.

I. Hall.

"The elements of the drawers can also join the waiting stack to allow them to air before dovetailing"

Making jigs

Mike uses two specially-made jigs for use on a table saw – a cross-cutting box and a jig for tenons. Mike's tenoning jig is similar to one found in Bob Wearing's book *Making Woodwork Aids and Devices*.

Tenon-cutting jig

Bob's version of a cutting jig is excellent for cutting the cheeks of tenons. It uses the mitre-guide slots on a table-saw, and is quite sophisticated in that it allows angled tenons to be cut. A simpler version could be made for 90° only operation.

The jig is constructed of birch ply with metal or wooden slides, with a clamp that can be made of either material. A slide allows the jig to be adjusted for different cuts and thicker tenons, and the stop can be made adjustable by drilling more than one set of holes in the vertical working face.

As the table saw's riving knife and crown guard have to be taken off for this jig, a separate guard will have to be made. A simple version is shown in Bob's book.

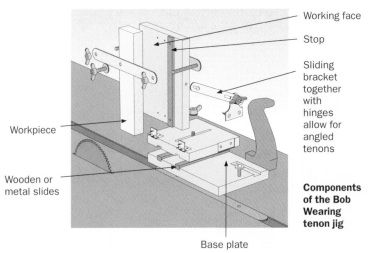

Working face

Stop

Sliding bracket together with hinges allow for angled tenons

Workpiece

Wooden or metal slides

Base plate

Components of the Bob Wearing tenon jig

Cross-cutting box

A cross-cutting box can be made using the bed slots of a table saw. This is also made from plywood – the size depends on your saw. Start with the runners; these should be made to fit slightly below the level of the table, so that when they are screwed to the base they will ride free of the bottom of the groove. Once cut to size, put the base board against the rip fence – this will make sure it is square to the bed slots – then with the runners in their slots mark out and drill the screw holes. Screw and glue the runners in place, then make the front and rear fences. Attach the front fence only and make your first cut; not all the way through though! Once it is cutting true you can fix the rear main fence.

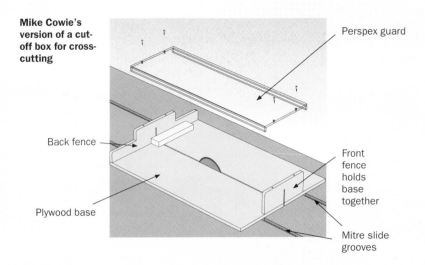

Mike Cowie's version of a cut-off box for cross-cutting

Perspex guard

Back fence

Front fence holds base together

Plywood base

Mitre slide grooves

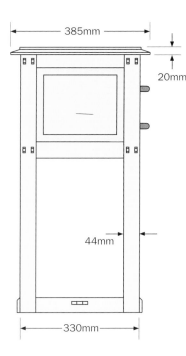

385mm

20mm

44mm

330mm

"Do a dry assembly to check for accuracy, and at the same time decide which is to be the front, so that the sides and back can be marked for grooving to accept the panels"

are driven home. Check for square and leave to dry.

I clean off any surplus glue whilst still rubbery and then clean up the wedges with a block plane and level the edges of the tenons.

Drawer construction

Much has been written about drawer construction and the cutting of dovetails, and whilst it would be nice to spend time and ensure that everything is perfect I, unfortunately along with many, work under the constraints of time and price. The pair of tables illustrated took 35 hours, but your work is judged by the quality or lack of it, and so time saved

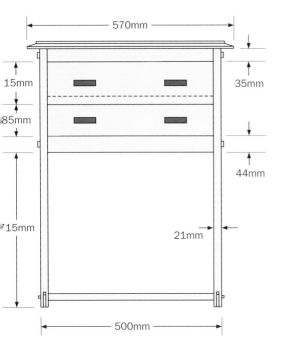

570mm

15mm

35mm

85mm

44mm

15mm

21mm

500mm

Top drawer detail showing overhang that covers the drawer rail

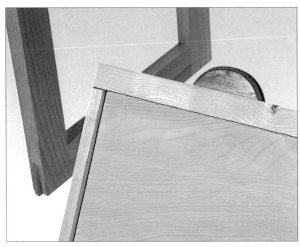

Cedar of Lebanon drawer bottoms always add something special to a piece

Drawer runner detail showing strip glued to give extra smooth operation

on other elements is spent trying to obtain a nice fitting drawer with good dovetails. Having said that, I always remember a comment made while I was at college: "Remember who you are making the piece for – it is the client, not to impress other makers". It is a pertinent point, but I still try to make my work as good as possible within the time constraint.

Drawer fronts

The drawer fronts were cut from a nicely figured piece of elm, with the intention of being a matched pair, and though white, and therefore sappy, this was not a problem. You will notice that

the top drawer has a lip to cover the drawer rail, which also acts as a stop.

I used cedar of Lebanon *(Cedrus libani)* for the drawer bottoms – a small piece gives that lovely sweet smell.

Top

The top comes last, and is planed, jointed and edged with a small inlay of padauk to balance the handles.

The handles are cut rough on the bandsaw and finished with a half round cutter via a small jig and the router.

The finish is dual – a French polish for the carcass and Danish oil for the top for added durability of the oil where spillages may occur. ■

Making Woodwork Aids & Devices
by Robert Wearing is published by
GMC Publications, price **£10.95**,
ISBN 1 86108 129 4
Available from:
GMC Publications Ltd,
166 High Street, Lewes,
East Sussex BN7 1XU
Tel: 01273 488005
Fax: 01273 478606

Ex-static design

Mark Ripley makes an extending dining table in American white oak

PHOTOGRAPHY BY MANNI CEFAI   ILLUSTRATION BY IAN HALL

ABOVE: Three-piece suite – the complete commission in situ

THIS TABLE was the second phase of a dining suite which also included a display dresser and six chairs. The chairs are the feature of the following article, but here we will concern ourselves with the table.

While a dresser takes between three and four weeks working full-time, a simple table can be made in as many days. My initial proposal was, in fact, for a static table, but subsequently the client felt that an extension to accommodate two additional places would be more appropriate.

It is tempting to under-charge for modifications to the brief once an estimate has been accepted – after all, no maker wants the fish slipping off the hook at the last minute; but what, to the uninitiated, seems like a modest request, may, as in the case of this table, virtually double the amount of time it will take to make. The answer is to explain the implications to the client, perhaps suggesting ways of making another aspect of the job more economical.

As it happens, we had already discussed a simpler format for the dresser base, so were halfway there. A modest increase in the overall cost covered the rest.

Design

Part of the process of design is the art of balancing numerous factors. These include the functional requirements of the piece, the visual

"When it comes to facing off wide boards, my belt sander and I have an understanding – we don't get on"

idea, proportion and detail, materials and craftsmanship. If any one of these becomes dominant at the expense of the others, the piece will lack harmony.

To me, the best work is not demanding, has poise and feeds the soul. These perceptions may be present both in work that is a quiet evolution of traditional themes and that which is radical and innovative.

The ends of the table top are very shallow semi-ellipses, relieving what would otherwise be a basic design. The edge of the top picks up the moulded detail of the dresser base, and the legs have stopped ovolo mouldings. A bead runs along the bottom edge of the frame.

> "Because 3in oak stock is liable to splits and honeycombing during the drying process – invisible until the board is opened up – allow for this when ordering"

Trying to store leaves inside a table frame can be a real headache, but is, nevertheless, quite possible for a single piece. In this case, however, the customer was happy that the leaf should be stored elsewhere.

The extension system itself involves each end of the top being fitted to two runners guided by notches in the table frame.

Table top
In preparing the cutting list the top takes precedence. Ideally selecting from a generous stock, the wood is planed and laid out. On static tables the grain usually runs along the top; in extending tables it runs across and in spite of the extra length the latter is probably easier.

Thirteen boards make up the top, which has an overall length of 2133mm (84in), with a single leaf 457mm (18in) wide.

Once the timber is planed and approximately dimensioned, the pieces are laid out. The aim is to create a top that is well balanced, whether open, with the leaf in place, or closed.

This is solid American white oak (*Quercus alba*), so the finished result will not look like veneered MDF and will probably produce more variation in colour and figure.

The second, and equally important factor, is structural balance. This is achieved by alternating the growth rings, neutralising the effect of radial shrinkage.

A simple check is to look at the wavy effect of the annual rings on the end of the assembled board. I have read that this is not all that important; all I can say is that I have always done it this way and never had a problem.

Arranging the boards to fulfil these requirements takes time and patience, so don't hurry. A brush and a pot of white spirit are very useful when checking what the finished colour will look like.

Preparation
Although my surface planer is very effective; I still finish the joints by hand with a No. 7 jointer to remove the ripples left by the machine.

The butt joints are fitted with biscuits, and the excess glue wiped off while it is still wet. Preparation is the key to successful woodworking – never more so than in the making up of wide boards.

Whatever technique is used to face off a jointed up board, a series of steps and wonky planks presents a problem. Well prepared joints and careful gluing up are 90% of the secret, the other 10% being, perhaps, a matter of personal preference.

For most of us the choice is between hand-planing or a portable belt sander. When it comes to facing off wide boards, my belt sander and I have an understanding – we don't get on.

My old Elu 3in sander with a sanding frame was a good intermediate machine, preparing a flat but untidy surface for hand-sanding. Unfortunately it finally gave out earlier this year, precipitating a major re-evaluation of my sanding system.

The Elu has been replaced by an orbital sander, while a 4in belt sander is used principally for preparing frames. For wide boards, I find hand-planing quicker, more accurate and more pleasant than belt-sanding.

> "Chamfering the bottom of the legs before assembly allows the foot to slide more easily over a carpet"

Frame
The frame is fairly straightforward. Because 3in oak stock is liable to splits and honeycombing during the drying process – invisible until the board is opened up – allow for this when ordering. Fortunately the legs do not require a great deal of stock.

Using pegs for extra strength, the rails are mortice and tenoned to the legs. As well as the end rails, a couple of central rails are also prepared. These may either be biscuit-jointed or stub tenoned.

The notches to guide the sliding rails must be marked out and cut prior to assembly.

The beads on the lower edge of the main rails were cut with a combination plane – quieter than a router.

Chamfering the bottom of the legs before assembly allows the foot to slide more easily over a carpet, thus greatly reducing the strain on the joints if the table is dragged across the floor.

Sliding mechanism

The tops are fitted to inverted T-section rails. In turn, these rails are screwed to rectangular-section rails, forming a cranked runner. The T-section part slides in a corresponding opening in the top of the table's end frames.

The rectangular components slide in notches in the bottom of the central

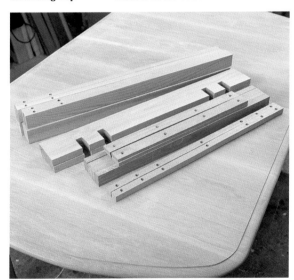

MOULDING THE LEGS

The legs are given a stopped moulding formed by using a ¼in shank ovolo router cutter with a ¼in radius. In order to achieve this, a simple jig must be made, consisting of two L-shaped stops which are placed at each end of the leg. These are made up with scraps of ply pinned and glued together, see *diagram*.

The jig pieces and a leg are then set up and held between bench dogs. An alternative, for those without a tail vice, is to clamp the leg in a conventional vice, using a sash cramp to hold the two pieces of the jig in place over the back of the leg and away from the side to be routed.

Once the mouldings have been routed, finish the ends of the moulding by carving the details with a fishtail gouge.

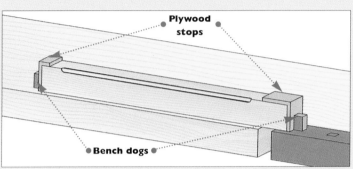

Plywood stops

Bench dogs

ABOVE: Simple ply pieces form a jig to rout the mouldings on the legs

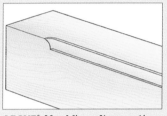

ABOVE: Moulding after routing

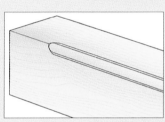

ABOVE: Detail carved in

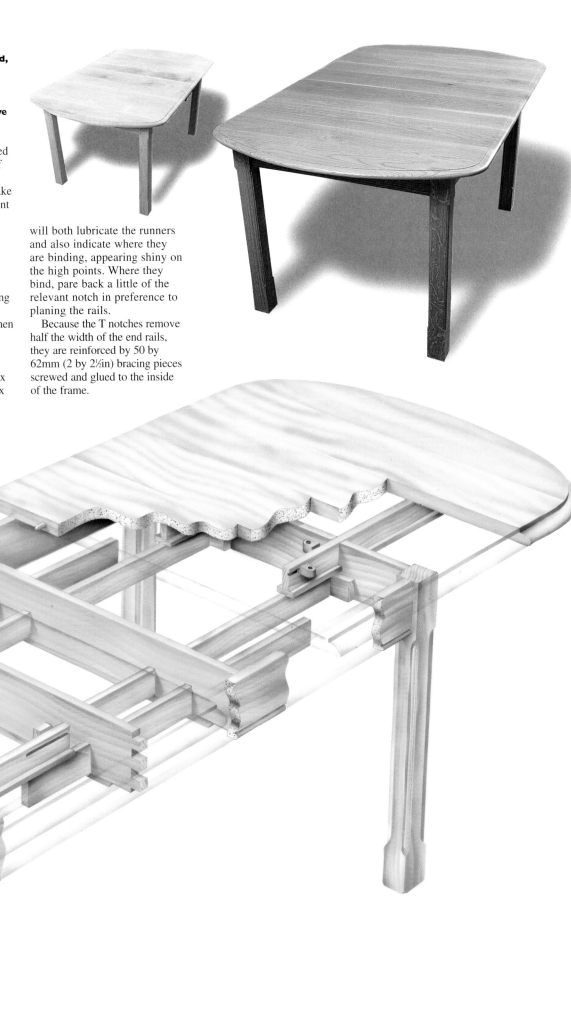

rails, and are retained by capping strips. Screws are fitted through the 'outboard' ends of the rails to hold the top. The 'inboard' end is morticed to take buttons, allowing for movement in the top.

The process of setting up the top to run smoothly takes up much of the time, the components themselves being straightforward.

Before putting the whole thing together, ensure that the rails slide in their respective slots, then assemble the cranked rails and check that they run freely and parallel to one another.

Finally, fit the tops and wax all the running parts. The wax will both lubricate the runners and also indicate where they are binding, appearing shiny on the high points. Where they bind, pare back a little of the relevant notch in preference to planing the rails.

Because the T notches remove half the width of the end rails, they are reinforced by 50 by 62mm (2 by 2½in) bracing pieces screwed and glued to the inside of the frame.

I. Hall

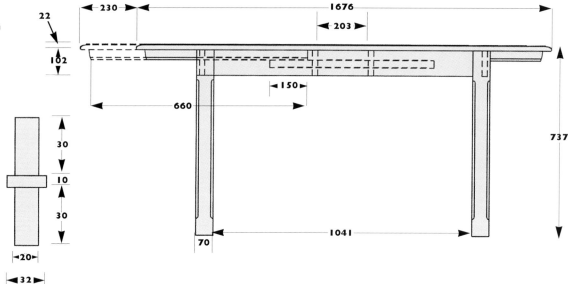

RIGHT: Front elevation and plan

22
102
30
10
30
|◄20►|
|◄32►|

Rail section

230
1676
◄203►
◄150►
660
737
1041
70

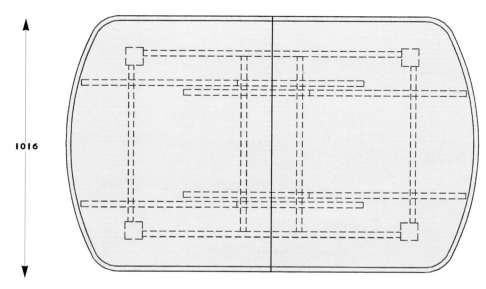

1016

Notches are offset to facilitate rails

MARK RIPLEY gained a BA (Hons) degree in Three Dimensional Design at Leicester Poly where he specialised in furniture design and making. For the next 10 years he divided his time between furniture-making and teaching woodwork to handicapped adults. For the past six years he has devoted all his time to designing and making furniture from a converted farm building at South Moreton, Oxfordshire.

Fit and finish

The tops locate and align with brass lugs. Connectors are necessary to hold the table top together – these may be of wood but the resulting effect is likely to be rather cumbersome. A much neater solution is found in hatch or locker catches, *see panel.*

The finish is Danish oil on a polyurethane sanding sealer. This is applied with a cloth, so do make sure you have a good stock of the lint-free variety to hand. Apply a thin coat each day for several days.

In the following article, Mark Ripley describes the making of his complementing set of chairs.

"Yacht chandlers stock a wide range of tasty fittings just waiting for an imaginative application to cabinet work"

CHANDLERY IS THE BUSINESS

Hatch and locker catches are available from yacht chandlers, and consist of a cam and lever which pull a D ring over a hook. Fittings of a similar description can be found in some hardware stores, but these tend to be lightweight pressed-steel affairs. The yachting variety are of heavy brass.

Incidentally, yacht chandlers stock a wide range of tasty fittings just waiting for an imaginative application to cabinet work. I recently discussed with one company the possibility of having some custom-made bronze fittings produced – another one of those ideas sitting on the back burner waiting for the right application.

Almost stock

Mark Ripley makes six chairs to complement his dining table

PHOTOGRAPHY BY MANNI CEFAI   MAIN ILLUSTRATION BY IAN HALL

A DINING TABLE, especially a simple one, can be very satisfying because of the relative speed at which a small number of components can be turned into a large and highly functional piece of furniture.

While chairs are no less functional, that is where the similarity ends; this traditionally based ladder back design is constructed from some 22 complex components.

Stock designs

The design process itself is time-consuming because a chair is not, like many cabinets, a series of two-dimensional faces; it is made up of compound angles and curves that are almost impossible to work out of paper.

Models may suffice for communicating the idea of sculptural forms in a cabinet, but chair design demands full-size prototypes; this is the only way to test for comfort.

A designer is unlikely to recoup the development costs of a new chair design in one commission, unless it is for a large number of chairs. Over the years I have developed two stock chair designs which are adjusted to suit.

"This is an exercise in batch production, with any mistakes multiplied"

Prototypes

These are constantly evolving, are never produced in the same way twice and provide a starting point from which I can make a prototype for each new generation.

This need not take long and may vary from a quick lash-up to check a visual idea to a pre-production prototype. The latter will include all

RIGHT: A fully jointed, full-size mock-up, the only way to test strength and comfort

"Needless to say it was the managing director's chair that collapsed, leaving him face to face with the maker's label"

joints and accurate dimensions, and be used as a three-dimensional working drawing.

These are made in softwood, usually with bandsawn surfaces, and are unfinished. The three or four in my workshop provide a useful talking point, as well as seating, for visitors. A number of times I have had to dissuade people from buying them – for one thing I find them useful and, secondly, I would hate

anyone to think that they represented the quality of my finished work.

A visiting lecturer at college told us to burn all our prototypes. One of his had accidentally been delivered with a consignment of boardroom chairs. Needless to say it was the managing director's chair which collapsed, leaving him face to face with the maker's label. He reached for the phone while still sitting on the floor.

> "In preparing the timber, make enough parts for an additional chair. This allows for natural defects and the odd...um...unnatural one"

The value of prototypes as part of the design process lies in working out the visual, ergonomic and structural aspects of a chair. I would also advocate their use when making a set of chairs to an established design, as they will familiarise the maker with their construction, aid the making of jigs and templates and provide a reference point.

Remember that this is an exercise in batch production, with any mistakes multiplied.

So for those unfamiliar with chair-making I would suggest the making of a finished softwood 'prototype' as a project in its own right.

Structure

The structure of this chair is conventional. Apart from four lower ladder 'rungs', all the joints are mortice and tenoned. Dowels may be an adequate alternative for an occasional chair but for dining chairs I would not advise them.

The four main sets of joints around the seat are reinforced with corner blocks.

When preparing the timber, make enough parts for an additional chair. This allows for natural defects and the odd...um...unnatural one.

The back legs are shaped and the mortices marked out. The corresponding mortices are marked on the front legs and the legs put into sets. This is important as there are right- and left-handed legs, so keeping them in order is imperative.

The mortice and tenon in the back leg is a compound joint, further complicated by being set in a curved rail. Cutting angled mortices in the legs is achieved by means of a jig, *see drawing*.

This holds the leg at an angle to the mortice chisel. A similar arrangement could be used on a bench drill, the joint being drilled out and cleaned up by hand. Double-check each cut to ensure that the mortice is angled in the right direction.

Side rails

The tenons for the side rails must all be marked out individually using a sliding bevel and square. Again, these are right- and left-handed and must be put in pairs. Concentrate on the top rails first as the stretchers are marked off later.

Although the cheeks may be cut on a bandsaw, take care not to run through the shoulder of the tenon, especially on the back leg joint. The remainder of the tenon is cut and finished by hand.

A small, flat area is planed over the back leg mortice. Thus the shoulder of the tenon fits onto a flat rather than a curved surface. The outside edge of the leg is sanded to a fair curve at a later stage.

Using a clamp to pull the joint up, assemble the front and back legs and top rail. Each assembly is checked with its partner and any necessary adjustments made to the tenon shoulders until each pair matches.

These top rails are a critical part of the job so must be accurate. The stretcher rails are scribed off the sides of the legs while they are still clamped up. These are marked, cut and checked in the same way as the top rails.

The front and back rails are all perpendicular to the legs, making the joints much easier to cut by machine. Remember, though, that the carvers are wider than the standard version.

The top rung of the ladder back should be mortice and tenoned, but the remainder are wide enough to take a size 00 biscuit. The joints are prepared on the top rung prior to cutting the curve.

A full dry assembly to check that everything fits probably needs to be done on one chair only. All the components are sanded, the legs are rounded over to a radius of 3mm (1/8in). An ovolo moulding is applied to the top of the back and the top edge of the rails.

> "For those unfamiliar with chair-making I would suggest the making of a finished pine 'prototype' as a project in its own right"

ABOVE: Morticed components stacked in handed pairs – very important!

ABOVE: Create a flat on the curved back leg for the tenon shoulders

ABOVE: Testing for fit – side rail tenon and back leg mortice

One approach...

A chair's back leg joints are the most important in the structure. They take an enormous amount of stress on a daily basis – and that's even before people do such monstrous things as leaning back on them.

So when designing chairs it is important to bear these factors in mind. The deeper you can make the tenon, the end grain component, the better its chances of surviving the racking forces of chair usage. It also increases the gluing area.

The conventional approach to the cutting of the back leg mortices and tenons in chairs used by most furniture makers is to angle the tenon and have a parallel mortice. Using this technique makes for easy setting up on the morticer, but can lead to tenons with short grain because of the angle at which they are cut – it pays to be careful when selecting timber for side rails.

Although some time will have to be spent making a jig for the tenons, this will soon amply reap rewards as most of us rarely make only one chair at a time.

...and another

On the other hand angling the mortice, which is Mark's approach, could take too much of the meat out of the leg, because of the slope of the mortice cutting across the thickness of the leg. Here he uses the largest possible corner blocks to supplement the inherent strength of the ladder structure of this back, making for a very strong chair.

As well as considering the joint in isolation it has to be weighed up alongside the whole structure of the back.

Mark uses angled blocks as jigs to achieve his desired mortice.

The front leg jig consists of simple, angled parallel blocks screwed together. The back leg jig is a little more complicated in that it is curved as well as angled; the back legs of the chair are marked with the angle of the mortice and then the mortice chisel is wound out past the leg and trued up with the line.

A small block under the jig makes adjustment easier; when tapped backwards or forwards it will raise or lower the jig.

All of this emphasises one of the

ABOVE: Back legs on the morticer – note angle and jig

reasons why it is important to make a full size mock up to test the joint.
Colin Eden-Eadon

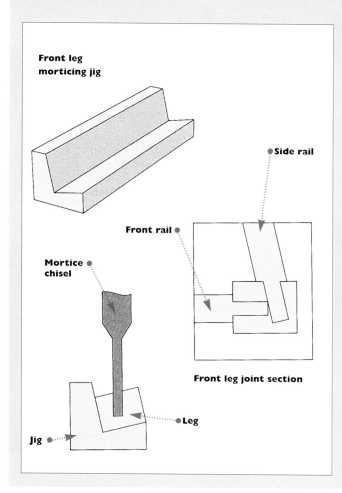

Front leg morticing jig

- Side rail
- Front rail
- Mortice chisel
- Leg
- Jig

Front leg joint section

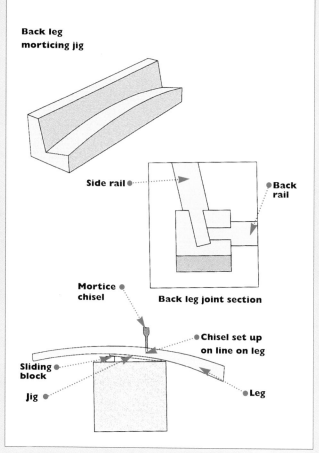

Back leg morticing jig

- Side rail
- Back rail

Back leg joint section

- Mortice chisel
- Chisel set up on line on leg
- Sliding block
- Jig
- Leg

I Hall

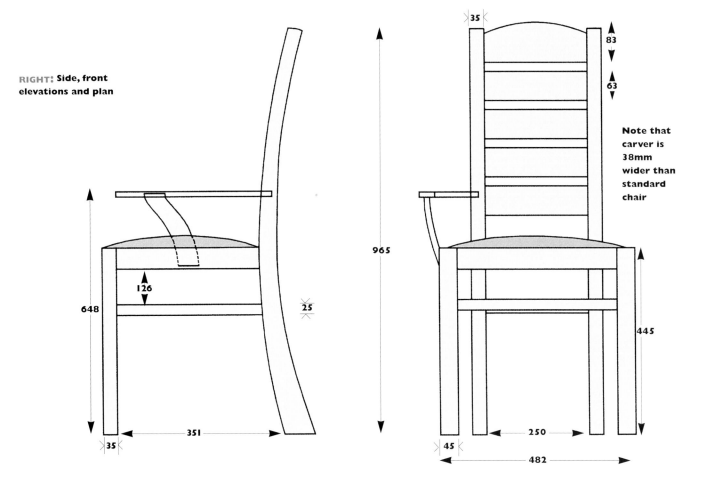

126

648

25

351

35

965

35

83

63

Note that carver is 38mm wider than standard chair

445

45

250

482

Assembly

The legs and side rails are glued up first and left in clamps overnight. These are particularly important joints and should be given every assistance. The rest of the chair must be glued up in one well-planned operation.

Corner blocks – as big as possible – are fitted below the top of the rail to reinforce the mortice and tenon joints and screwed into place.

If carvers are being made, the arms and supports may now be prepared. The shapes of these components are quite complex. Right- and left-hand softwood patterns help to resolve these, and also act as templates for the actual job.

The arms are joined to the back legs with stub tenons. A screw is used to give the joint more strength, the hole being counterbored and filled with a pellet. The arm support is fitted to the chair rail with a halving joint and, like the stub tenon, screwed and plugged. The arm and its support are joined with a mortice and tenon joint.

All of the many joints in each chair must be checked for glue marks before they are finished. Brushing on white spirit reveals light patches where excess glue needs to be scraped off.

The chairs are sealed with 70/30 polyurethane/white spirit, burnished with wire wool and Danish oiled.

The drop-in seat panels are made from 9mm birch ply, and are individually fitted and numbered. An allowance of 2mm should be left all the way round the seat panel, after the edges have been rounded over, for the upholstery. Even though this is a relatively straightforward job, I always use professionals for the upholstery. They have the expertise and access to materials at trade prices, and for a one-off chair may offer you an offcut of fabric.

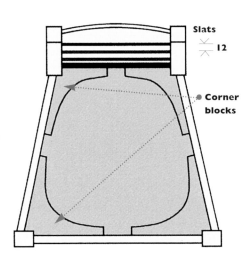

Slats

12

Corner blocks

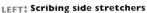

LEFT: Scribing side stretchers

RIGHT: Main parts dry assembled, awaiting biscuit-jointed back slats

Birth of the

Norman Speller describes the trials and tribulations of making a competition-winning table

● **Having attending a two-year foundation course at art college, NORMAN SPELLER has worked as a carpenter and joiner for the past eighteen years on anything from roofs to bank counters. In the near future he hopes to set up his own workshop, designing and making quality furniture**

BELOW: Walnut, chrome and slate made for a winning combination at the first Axminster show

ON FLICKING THROUGH my copy of *Furniture and Cabinetmaking* one day last summer I came across a page that made me stop – it heralded the first ever *F & C* furniture competition at the Axminster Tool and Machinery Exhibition. Like many makers, I had hankered after exhibiting my work, but had never found the opportunity, until now. There was a lot to consider – was my work up to scratch, were my designs good enough, could I make something in time? The line-up of judges was formidable.

After a few nail-biting weeks I plucked up the courage and sent off for an application form.

The design

The piece that I decided to make for the show was a development of a table I had made some years ago. I find it fascinating to look back at past work, knowing that if you use the idea again, it will be quite different. And so it was with my new piece.

I wanted the table to be bold. After a number of drawings it became apparent that this was just what it was, and that it would be the kind of piece to go in the reception area of a corporate company, or a luxury apartment overlooking the Thames. I called it the MK 2.

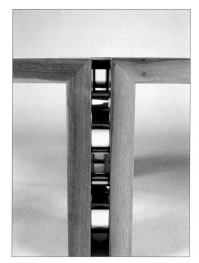

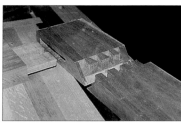

ABOVE: Detail of chrome rings connecting legs
TOP RIGHT: Components of top and legs with tenon and mitred secret dovetails
ABOVE RIGHT: Simple jig using guide bush and dovetail cutter to cut dovetails on infill pieces

'Working as a carpenter and joiner does have its benefits – I was able to use the company workshop, which is just as well, as mine is still under construction at the bottom of the garden"

MK2

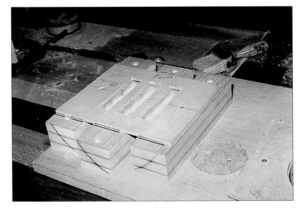

"Time was tight – from the start I only had about five weeks to finish the piece, and there were times when I just didn't think that I was going to make it"

The materials

It was to be a quite splendid affair in comparison to its predecessor. I chose American black walnut (*Juglans nigra*) for its rich figure, which I intended to exploit, and, at this point, the top was to be made of glass. In the closing weeks this changed dramatically – not a move I recommend! *See panel.*

Time was tight – from the start I only had about five weeks to finish the piece, and there were times when I just didn't think that I was going to make it.

Down to business

Working as a carpenter and joiner does have its benefits – I was able to use the company workshop, which is just as well, as mine is still under construction at the bottom of the garden.

The walnut was no problem, a local timber merchant was most helpful. But the four-inch copper tube required for the legs proved to be a nightmare. I spent days phoning suppliers, in what little spare time I had, until bingo! A local chroming company had a six foot length left over from a previous job. A price was agreed and the copper purchased.

I explained my intention of cutting the tube into rings which would require chroming and they were happy to undertake the work for £20, promising that it could be completed in a day.

The joinery

The joinery for this piece is straightforward. Where the legs meet the top timber a mitred dovetail is used, but there is a tendency to forget that this table has eight legs, and mitred dovetails can take time.

The chrome rings on the legs posed a problem as I did not want to show any form of fixings. The way I got round this, is that each ring has a timber infill with a twin dovetail to each face – with this arrangement the face side of each leg has a corresponding morticed dovetail that can take two forms.

In the first method, the dovetail pins to the timber infill will need to taper, as will the mortice – remember to allow for the pin to fit into the corresponding mortice, which would then slide, and lock into position. The pin length must be shorter than the mortice.

The second method is where the dovetail pins remain parallel as do the corresponding mortices, but in this case the length of the mortice is divided equally into four, with alternate sections being enlarged to take the full width of the dovetail pins. The pins are also divided into the same four equal sections with the first section being removed and the remaining mid-section pin being reduced in width to the size of the pin's base – the two pieces will go together, slide, and become locked.

I chose to use the second method, but you have to remember to assemble the joint in the correct way, if not, the mortice will be exposed.

With the use of a router, guide bush, and jigs, the job is made much quicker. Two simple jigs are needed, one to cut the dovetails using a TCT two-flute dovetail cutter. The other is used to trim the infill to a true circle, using a straight flute cutter.

Rout the dovetails first as the blank blocks will be easier to hold while square. The infills can be bandsawn to an oversize circle first and then trimmed or routed from square.

I screwed both jigs to a base board – this meant no clamps got in the way when routing. I also routed two dovetail slots in the base board to take the infill once the first pair of tails had been cut – this made holding them in the jig a lot easier.

Lastly double mortice and tenons with a haunch in the middle are used to lock the top pieces together.

BELOW: **Jig and first routed dovetails**

BOTTOM: **Infill with both sides' dovetails routed**

"After a few nail-biting weeks I plucked up the courage and sent off for an application form"

Final run

With thirty hours to go I had everything I needed, the walnut was oiled and waxed – and all I had to do was assemble the table.

On the morning of 13th November I set out at 5.30am so as to avoid the London traffic and arrived safe and sound at the Royal Bath and West Showground, Shepton Mallet, Somerset at 9.30am.

I booked in my entry and decided to check out the competition. By that time only six or seven pieces had arrived, but the quality of the work was exceptional. I exchanged a few words with Quentin Jaume, who was also entering the competition with his table and chair, and, having wished him luck, I set off for the long drive home.

I'd done it! What a relief it was after all the hard work of the past few weeks – the sense of satisfaction was indescribable!

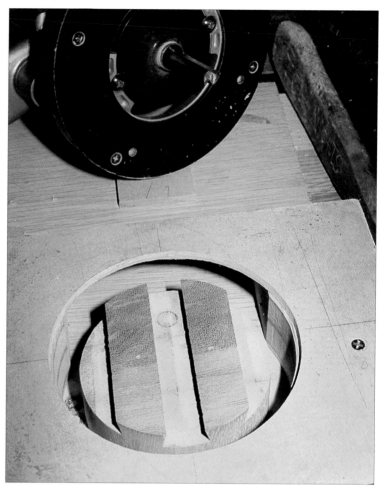

"With thirty hours to go I had everything I needed, the walnut was oiled and waxed – and all I had to do was assemble the table"

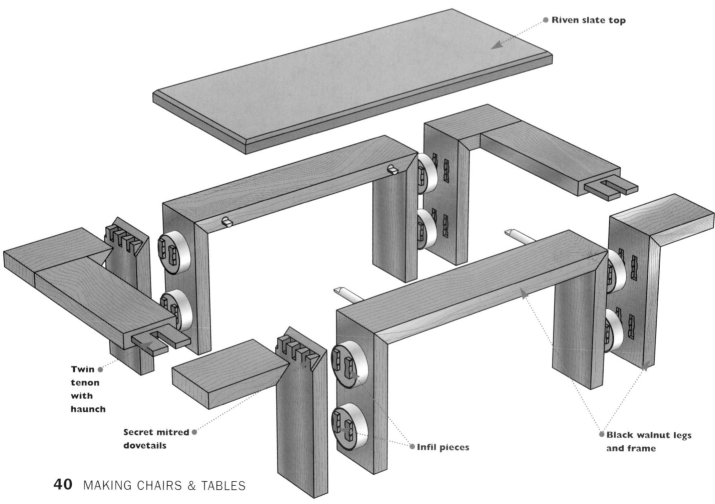

Riven slate top

Twin tenon with haunch

Secret mitred dovetails

Infil pieces

Black walnut legs and frame

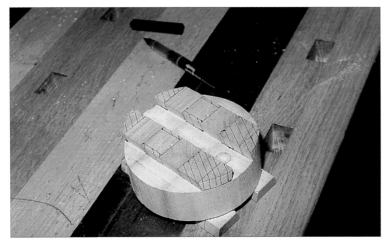

> "There is a tendency to forget that this table has eight legs, and mitred dovetails can take time"

TOUCH AND GO

I had never been altogether happy about using glass for the table top, and with only two weeks to go I decided to use slate instead. I had no idea if the size would be a problem or even whether it was feasible.

The finish I was after is known as riven, which is where the slate is split to thickness by its natural grain.

So it was back to the phone. It didn't take long to discover that riven finish is not popular and is difficult to find. Finally I stumbled across a north London stonemason who suggested that it might be possible to split some 30mm China slate after it had been cut to size. This would have to be done by hammer and chisel, and it was a long shot – but with time running out I had little option but to give it a try.

But this wasn't my only problem. I was having trouble with the chroming – I'd been told that the work could be completed in one day but when I went to pick it up on 5th November I was told it would take a week. They agreed to finish it by 11th November, but now wanted £5 for each ring – the price had doubled!

The final week

It was all getting a bit touch and go.

On returning to the stonemason I was told that he was having problems. The grain of the slate was not running parallel with the machined surface. It was asking a lot to take 5 to 10mm off the top of a 400 to 900mm piece of slate.

Now this seemed like a good time to go into panic mode, but us carpenters are made of sterner stuff.

It was the weekend and I had to wait until Monday to get back to the phone. With only three days to go I had to find a stonemason who could carry out the work.

On Monday morning I managed to track down John Fouracres, who is a specialist in marble, granite, and slate, and explained my problem.

John had just what I needed – Italian slate. Although very busy, he was willing to help. All I had to do was get a template, of the size required, to him before 7.00am on Tuesday. I could collect the finished slate before the close of business that day.

All went well, John did a great job and I picked up the slate the following afternoon. I needed to collect the chroming on my way home and, as luck would have it, I got caught in a traffic jam – with minutes to spare I made it!

This cabinetmaking business certainly gets the adrenalin going!

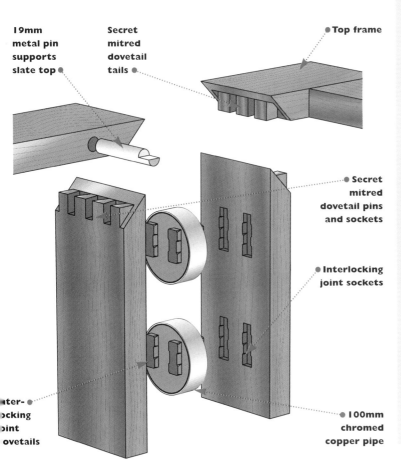

19mm metal pin supports slate top •

Secret mitred dovetail tails •

• Top frame

• Secret mitred dovetail pins and sockets

• Interlocking joint sockets

•ter- •
ocking
oint
ovetails

• 100mm chromed copper pipe

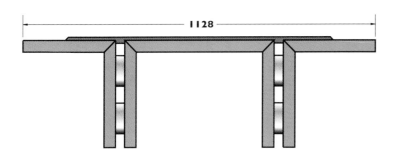

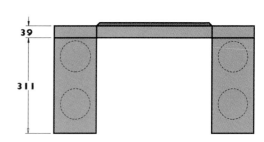

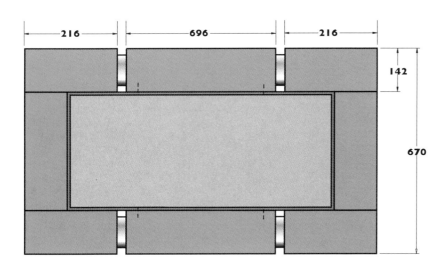

"I needed to collect the chroming on my way home and, as luck would have it, I got caught in a traffic jam – with minutes to spare I made it!"

A phone call

Two days later, I received a phone call from Andrea Hargreaves at *F&C* to inform me that my entry had come second place in the Amateur category. Not in my wildest dreams had I thought of winning – I couldn't believe my ears! But sure enough, when I went to the show on the Sunday to collect my table, I was included in the prize-giving.

My hours of hard work, and the six hundred mile drive, had been worth it!

"It was the weekend and I had to wait until Monday to get back to the phone. With only three days to go I had to find a stonemason who could carry out the work"

BELOW LEFT: **Dry fit of joints and rings on legs**
BELOW RIGHT: **Socket part of locking dovetail joint**

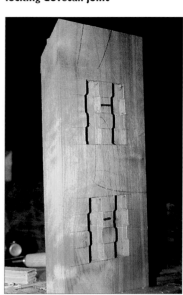

On leaving the RAF in 1987 **Kevin Ley** set to turning his hobby into a commercial proposition. The former squadron leader designs and makes bespoke furniture from his cottage and workshop in the wilds of Shropshire

Very simple, very country

In the final part of a kitchen refit, **Kevin Ley** makes a table and chairs

Last but not least

PHOTOGRAPHY BY THE AUTHOR
ILLUSTRATIONS BY SIMON RODWAY

I've just made a kitchen dresser for a client who, like me, prefers a mixture of fitted and free-standing kitchen furniture. Her's was a modern house in Yorkstone in a small, pretty village in Yorkshire, and she had achieved a nice blend of modern, functional, fitted units, with some traditional free standing pieces from me. The major free-standing piece was the large dresser in local elm (*Ulmus sp*). The client wanted a table and chairs in a different native hardwood but one sympathetic to that piece.

Timber prep

After some deliberation my client chose native ash (*Fraxinus sp*) for this project. This wood is cream to pale tan in colour, with a dark, sound, heartwood. It's tough, with a straight, coarse, open grain, and the figure is quite similar to the wych elm (*Ulmus glabra*) I had used in the dresser. To add interest to the table top I had some olive ash, which is the light to dark brown heartwood colour all over, with a marbled effect similar to Mediterranean olive wood (*Oleaceae sp*).

All this timber had been seasoned for sometime in my timber store, so its moisture content wasn't a problem, and I felt the construction would allow swelling or shrinking movement without noticeable effect. The main area of concern was all the stresses in the timber, stabilised before construction. To this end, all the pieces for the table top and chair seats were dimensioned slightly over size, sticked and stacked in the workshop. The stacks were initially

either weighted on top or put in clamps, so the tresses stabilised, after cutting the fibres to size it. The weights were removed, and the clamps slackened over a couple of weeks to ensure the pieces were all stable. A small amount of wind on the top or seat would alter the length of the legs!

Table top

This is made from four pieces: the centre pieces from olive ash and the two outside pieces of ordinary white ash (*Fraxinus americana*). The figure is carefully matched, running through the join to mask it – the overall effect is like a wide through and through board of ash with a lot of heart!

The edges of the boards are planed on the jointer and finished by hand to

Design

The brief was for something a bit different: simple, solid, and very 'country'. The table had to be as big as possible, without getting in the way, and could seat four adults. It so happened I was friendly with a local butcher based in the village and to whom I'd taken the odd pig to be prepared for the freezer – in my 'Good Life' days of attempted self-sufficiency.

His butcher's block – which had a top about 610 by 150mm (2ft by 6in) square and was a massive 305mm (12in) thick with four legs hammered straight into holes in the underneath – sprang to mind, and became the inspiration for the table. The top of a butcher's block is often end grain up to give better recovery from chopping and cutting. The depth of the top is to stop it splitting through, and to provide serious weight, to resist the forces applied to it.

We decided to make a stylised version with a fairly thick top, but with a normal 'long grain up' top, and collars to fix the legs. To keep the table user-friendly in the limited space available in the kitchen, the corners and edges were rounded off. The legs were refined a little by making them octagonal rather than square, in cross section.

The chairs were a logical progression, incorporating influences from a milking stool and an antique spinning chair I'd been asked to repair by some friends. The same rounding over was applied to the seat and back shape and edges. The legs fitted directly into the seat, with a fox wedge, and the back was held in position by pegs under the seat.

It's worth bearing in mind the dimensions of the table only just allow it through a standard 760mm (30in) doorway with the door off; so it was worth checking the entry route and restrictions before starting work!

Above: Side view of the table

Right: Front view of chair

"The brief was for something a bit different: simple, solid, and very 'country'. The table had to be as big as possible, without getting in the way, and could seat four adults"

remove the ripples. The centre of the join is left slightly hollow – when they are pulled up in the clamps this would cause extra pressure on the ends – allowing for the extra shrinkage as the ends dry out more than the centre. The joins are reinforced with double biscuits, and all is glued up with Cascamite, clamped checked for wind, and left to set. The diagonals are marked on the underside to enable the leg fixing collars to be positioned.

The corners are rounded off to a 150mm (6in) radius on the band saw and finished with a belt and drum sander. The top and bottom edges are rounded over using a 12mm (1/2in) bearing guided radius cutter in a hand held router.

Leg collars

Scrap pieces of 45 by 165 by 165mm (1³/4 by 6¹/2 by 6¹/2in) ash are used to make the collars to attach the legs to the top. The diagonals are marked to find the centre, and the screw fixing holes are drilled on these diagonals.

A 50mm (2in) hole saw is used to prduce the angled hole for the legs. The angle is found by drawing the table side and end cross-sections, full size, on hardboard and making ply angle setters. These are pieces of ply cut to the correct fixed angle, taken from the full-size drawing and used to set the angle of the work to the drill.

Then a jig is made to raise one corner of the collars to the correct height so the holes drilled by the perpendicular pillar drill are at the correct angle, giving the required splay on the table legs.

Legs

The legs are cut 25mm (1in) too long and planed 55mm (2¹/2in) square. The planer fence is set to 45° and the corners planed off to make the octagonal cross section. The tops of the legs are turned on the lathe to to fit the holes. If a lathe is not available they can be pared with a spoke shave. A saw cut is then made in the top of each leg, at right angles to the line of the grain on the collar, and a wedge made of some scrap oak to fit.

Top biscuit jointed

Collar glued and screwed

Tenon pegs

Back tenons

Octagonal legs

Wooden leg collar

Fox wedged tenons

The legs are finished down to 240 grit with a random orbital sander. Cascamite glue is then applied to the inside of the holes, and the leg tops pushed through until the low side is flush with the top surface of the collar; the wedge tapped home, and the glue left to set.

With the glue set, the tops of the legs are planed flush with the top surface of the collars. The collared legs are then positioned on the underside of the table top using the diagonal lines marked on the collars and the table top to locate them accurately, and dry fitted with screws only. The table is stood on a known level surface – I have a 1830 by 1220mm (6 by 4ft) piece of 25mm (1in) MDF, levelled as a reference surface – on the floor of the workshop.

Draw a line on each face of the leg by placing a 150mm (6in) metal rule on the level surface, and drawing a line along its top onto the leg which is parallel to the floor. A line parallel to this is drawn in the correct position, and the legs removed and trimmed to correct length on the bandsaw.

The legs are then glued and screwed into position, with the grain in the collars running in the same direction as the grain in the table top. If there are any access problems for the assembled table, leave out the glue and increase the number of screws so the legs are detachable.

Once the legs are fitted, the table top is finished down to 240 grit.

Chair seats

The rectangles of 32mm (1¹/4in) ash are cut for the chair seats. The positions of the holes for the legs are then marked and holes 25mm (1in) in diameter and 25mm (1in) deep, drilled for the legs. Then, using the same method for the table legs, gauges are cut from ply to set the angle of the work to the drill, and jigs made to repeat the holes for all eight front and back legs. A Forstner bit is used, its centre pin is short and would not penetrate the seat top surface.

A router, with a chock under one side of the base plate to set the correct angle, is used to cut the two 25 by 63mm(1 by 2¹/2in) through mortices for the back.

The seat is then shaped with a 100mm (4in) radius cut on the front corners, and a 150mm (6in) radius on the rear. The top and bottom edges are rounded over with a 12mm (¹/2in) bearing guided router cutter, and the seats finished to 240 grit.

Legs

The legs are cut 25mm (1in) over length and the octagonal cross section formed on the planer. To fit the holes in the seat, the top 32mm (1¹/4in) is turned on the lathe. I use a fox wedge in the top of the leg to ensure a tight fit. A saw cut is then made in the top 20mm (³/4in) of the leg and a wedge made to spread the join when the leg is hammered home. This wedge must be very accurate – just a tad wider than the saw cut – and nearly parallel so it will go right in, spreading the leg end to a tight fit, but not binding on the bottom of the hole; so preventing it going into its full depth. I think modern glues make just as strong a job, without the uncertainty and complication of the fox wedge,

Underside of table, showing leg collars

My own set made some time ago – showing the back tenon pegs

Cleaning up the glue on the chair legs

particularly the gap filling ones – not that I've ever had a loose joint in my life!

Certainly, my more recent versions have been glued up with Bison from Adquick; it has the added advantage of setting in about 10 minutes at normal temperatures, and reassuringly foaming out of the join to let you know it is full. When set, the foam is slightly compressible, allowing slight movement without breaking the bond. Any surplus is easily cut away with a sharp chisel. Alternatively, the hole can be drilled right through the seat and a normal wedge used in the top of the leg. When wedging any tenon, make sure the wedge line is at right angles to the grain run around the hole or mortise, to avoid splitting!

Once the legs are finished, fitted, and set, the seat is stood on the bench, and the legs trimmed parallel to length, in a similar manner to the table legs. The bottom of the legs are marked by placing a 12mm (1/2in) high, short straight edge against each face of the leg, and drawing a pencil line parallel with the

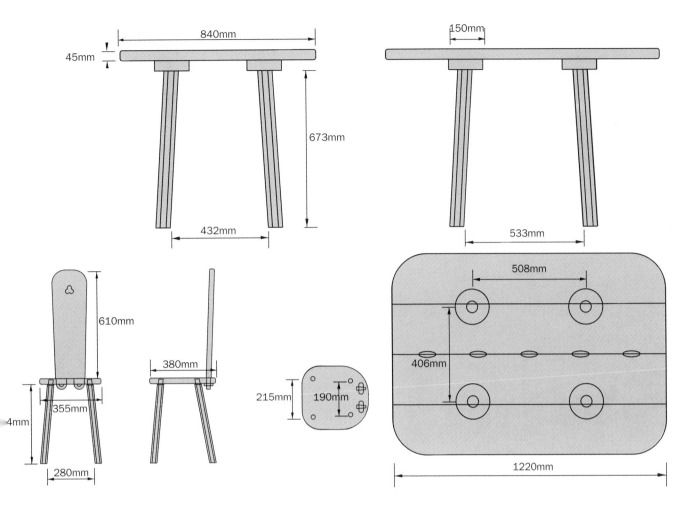

bench top, on the top edge. A line is drawn parallel in the correct position and the cut made on the bandsaw.

Backs

The backs are cut from 25mm (1in) ash. Before any shaping took place, the end tenons are cut and fitted through. With the tenons in position in the seat, the 3mm (1/8in) shoulder is marked – similar to the way the legs are trimmed – by placing a straight edge on the seat and drawing a line on the top edge. The actual cut line is marked parallel to this line, in the correct place. The cut is made with a tenon saw and planed flush to the remainder of the tenon with a shoulder plane. The bottom edge of the seat is marked on the tenons, and the 25mm (1in) peg holes drilled with their centres just inside the mortice, above the bottom line of the seat.

Pegs are made by turning 30mm (1 1/8in) dowels on the lathe and splitting them in half, down the length, on the band saw. The resultant half-round pegs are trimmed and pared to fit,

finally trimmed to length when they've been hammered home. The ends of the tenons are rounded to give a 20mm (3/4in) edge around the peg holes.

Shamrock finger hole

The three over lapping holes are drilled in the back with the 25mm (1in) forstner bit to form the shamrock shape. A pillar drill is used and the holes drilled from both sides to avoid breakout. This feature is not only decorative but gives a useful finger grip for lifting the chairs. Finally, the back is shaped on the bandsaw, finished with the belt sander, and the edges rounded over, using the 12mm (1/2in) bearing guided cutter in the router. It's finished and fixed in position, with the pegs hammered home, and trimmed to size.

Finish

The assembled table and chairs are finally hand finished down to 320 grit. and wiped over with white spirit prior to varnishing.

Five thin coats of satin finish polyurethane varnish are applied with a

sponge pad, and allowed to build up to a smooth finish. Each coat is allowed to dry for 24 hours in my warm dry workshop. The first two coats are cut back with 320 grit on a hard sanding block to allow the grain to fill. Further coats are cut back with a Scotchbrite grey pad to give a soft sheen. Although the final coat is dry in 24 hours or so it's better left for seven to 10 days to cure fully before use. The end result is a very durable, wipe clean, easy-to-maintain finish.

Conclusion

I've made several sets of these kitchen tables and chairs over the years, in a range of woods and finishes. It's a simple, useful project which is easily modified to give an individual touch. My favourite is a set I made in sycamore (*Acer pseudoplatanus*) with an unsealed table top which is simply scrubbed clean and bleached occasionally to remove difficult stains and to keep it hygienic. This was, of course, the norm for kitchen tables in the past, and looks and feels quite distinctive.

David Applegate, a member of the Somerset Guild of Craftsmen, served 16 years in the Royal Air Force as an aircraft engineer. In 1992 he became a self-employed furniture designer-maker, after studying at John Makepeace Summer Schools under Robert Ingham. Commissions have included 10 gallery seats for the Royal Botanic Gardens, Kew in 1990. David has successfully exhibited at the Celebration of Craftsmanship in Cheltenham and recently at the Martock Gallery

These tables were inspired by Richard William's winning versions at Axminster, 1998

Sweet inspiration

PHOTOGRAPHY BY ANTHONY BAILEY
ILLUSTRATIONS BY SIMON RODWAY

David Applegate makes two side tables in English walnut – part one

The F&C Furniture Exhibition at the Axminster Power Tools Show at Shepton Mallet must every year be a source of inspiration and example to many a designer-maker. Certainly, the 1998 show inspired me to consider the design and construction of a pair of side tables similarly sized to the winner of the Professional Class. Not to copy the design, but simply interpret what I saw in my own way.

I had been invited to exhibit at the 1999 Celebration of Craftsmanship Exhibition, Cheltenham, and I visualised the tables as a suitable foil to counterpoint the other two pieces, a small drawer chest and a longish low table. All the pieces were to be made of European walnut (*Juglans regia*) which I find the most rich looking timber of all – never mind the exotics from the rain forests!

Detail design

Now ideas were crystallising and the overall form of the project was taking shape, the detail design could begin...

When drawing up a project it's important to have the drawing to scale. This sounds obvious, I know, but experienced makers sometimes assume an original work can be produced without having put their ideas on paper, to scale, of the intended finished piece. Of course, the temptation is always there, but to be lazy at this stage is to deny the client or buyer the best results possible and sells the maker short, too.

Upon completing the drawing, as so often happens, the design looked 'slabby', too rectangular, and without originality. The muse had not visited! After a critical review, the legs became not just octagonal but fluted; the table edges were simplified

Luscious burr walnut veneer on the top

to a gentle inward slope and the cross-braces moved up to about two thirds of the leg height, instead of at half. Also, a centre boss would be an offcut from a leg, replicating the fluting provided where the cross-braces met.

Brainstorming

There would be a small drawer under the table top – not too large, in case the table became top-heavy – and this would require the palest sycamore (*Acer pseudoplatanus*) for the sides and base. I resolved to provide a dustboard, also in sycamore, under the drawer, to give a finished appearance to the underside. And herein lie two of my basic design principles: make the hidden detail of a contrasting material, to give a visual 'shock' when the interior is revealed, and always make the usually hidden sides and undersides of a piece of furniture properly presentable. Makers cannot possibly know exactly how a buyer will wish to use the piece, so all options should be suggested in the design and finishing.

Again, referencing sources of inspiration in design, the previous year at Cheltenham featured a piece with the finest scratch-stock work I'd ever seen. I decided to include this form of decoration in the tables, not to any excess but as a slight, understated hint which is how artificial decoration should always be. After all, the appeal of a piece of work should rest on the plain truth stated by the grain and colour of the timber and by the line and form of the design, although a little help may sometimes be acceptable.

Another feature I wanted to include was a burr walnut veneer on the top outlined in ebony (*Diospyrus ebenum*) inlay. I left the form, material and size of the drawer handles at this early design stage – they're much too important to be dogmatic about too early!

Side and back of table

An octagon is a convenient shape to make a square framework – the sides, back and front members can be jointed strongly into the legs in a very natural way. This construction renders mounting drawers a little difficult, though, because a plain drawer housing, with runners and kickers, would make the top heavy. I decided the drawers would be side-hung on very dry oak (*Quercus sp*) bearers. This way, I could avoid having drawer kickers just under the table top and thus I could easily fit buttons to hold the top to the carcass.

Table top design

The table tops themselves were to be finished with burr walnut (*Juglans sp*). This required a smooth, stable baseboard, not too heavy and not too thick – 16mm (⅝in) MDF fitted the bill – with a balancing veneer on the underside as the solution to the support for the show wood veneer.

Although I said earlier that all parts of a piece should be presentable, clearly the parts most on show must be afforded the best parts of the grain as far as possible. Adjacent pieces should have continuity in grain pattern and colour, so as not to jar the eye and alarm the sensibilities of the observer. This applies particularly to the drawer. The rails and the fronts should be cut from the same piece, so the actual drawer outline will show as thin dark lines only, then the buyer or observer only gradually becomes aware, as a mild surprise, there is a drawer. Subtlety also applied to the shaping of the components of the carcass; the undersides were not straight, but very slightly concave.

Having completed the design drawings, with a mental picture of how to make the tables, the construction can begin according to the cutting list made up from the drawing.

Construction

This is the stage when any 'bought out' parts should be ordered and obtained. If what's needed cannot be obtained, there will be sufficient time to alter the design to suit what is available! In this case, all that needed to be obtained from outside is European walnut burr veneer and I was lucky to locate a good supply of excellently figured stuff at Crispins, London, EC2, together with some first class advice and a supply of 4mm (⁵⁄₃₂in) ebony stringing. After inspection upon receipt, the veneer was returned to the transit packing and stored flat until needed. Another first job is to consider the legs because they are quite long in relation to their width. Straight, clear lengths of timber are first selected, cut out, squared and thicknessed about 8mm (⁵⁄₁₆in) oversize. They're stored vertically in a warmish, well ventilated part of the

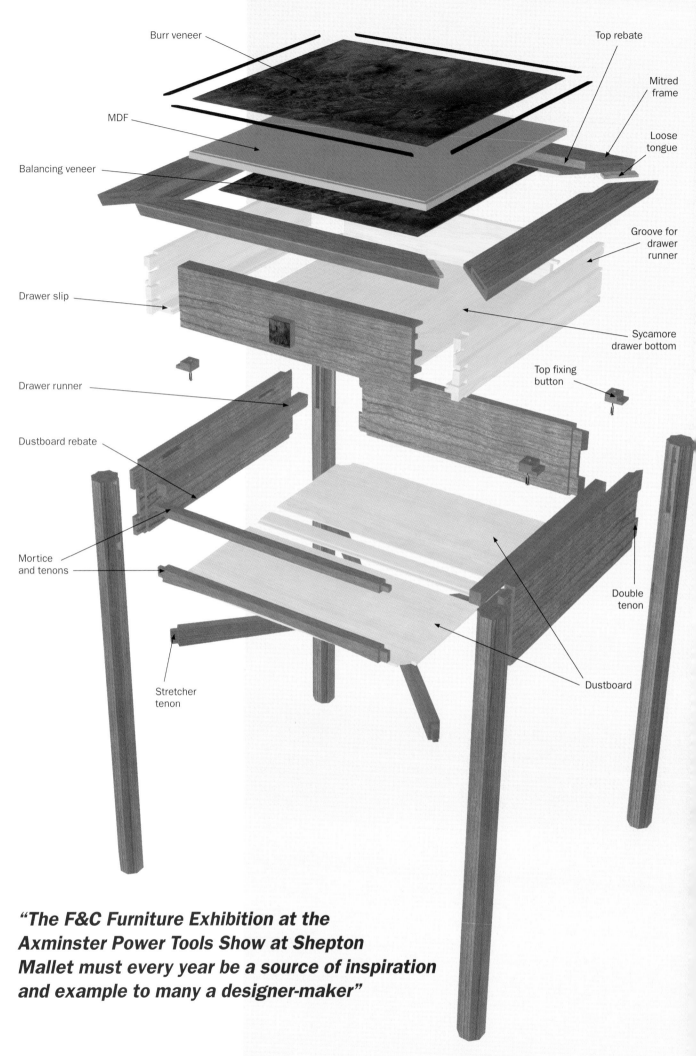

Burr veneer

MDF

Balancing veneer

Drawer slip

Drawer runner

Dustboard rebate

Mortice
and tenons

Stretcher
tenon

Top rebate

Mitred
frame

Loose
tongue

Groove for
drawer
runner

Sycamore
drawer bottom

Top fixing
button

Double
tenon

Dustboard

*"The F&C Furniture Exhibition at the
Axminster Power Tools Show at Shepton
Mallet must every year be a source of inspiration
and example to many a designer-maker"*

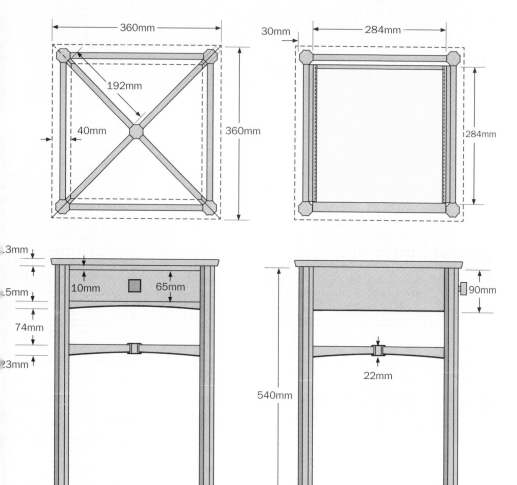

Fluting detail on the leg

"Makers cannot possibly know exactly how a buyer will wish to use the piece, so all options should be suggested in the design and finishing"

shop pending completion of the remaining parts of the carcass.

Tops

The first step in making the table tops is to form the frame surrounds for the edges. Well figured material is preferable here to complement the burr in the middle, remembering grain continuity in adjacent pieces is desirable. The frame is mitred together at the corners with a spline long enough to span the 45° angle of the mitre but stopping just short of the outer corners, to avoid break-out. As with all joints where there is a chance of an air space – such as mortices cut with a router, filled by a square-cut tenon – use Cascamite glue. PVA glues need air to cure, whereas Cascamite goes off in a settled void with no trouble.

The MDF should be suitably rebated into this surround, using the top face as

the datum, because it's important the veneered MDF sits uniformly flush with the face of the surround. Once glued in there's precious little scope for planing or sanding flush as the veneer is only 0.8 mm thick! The task of veneering is simplified greatly by using a vacuum extraction system. It's clean, uniform in pressure application and quick. If such a facility is not to hand, the foot square pieces in this project can be managed with G-clamps and thickish pieces of wood – remember to get as much pressure in the central parts as on the periphery, using slightly convex bearers, and use lots of polythene sheet, spread out smoothly.

It's a bit too much of an adventure trying to put the balance veneer on at the same time as the show wood, and the safe way is to put the balancer on first. PVA is ideal for this application: dampen

off the veneer a little and dilute the PVA very slightly – enough to make it flow visibly faster, no more, and spread with a serrated plastic spreader. When the glued assembly is dry, set aside safely, to avoid damage to the veneer. A dull sheen on the surface of the veneer may be apparent at this stage though don't worry as it's only excess glue forced up through the veneer and will smooth itself out on the underside of the polythene sheet layer used to keep the work clear of the wooden supports. The sheen will disappear when the veneer is sanded later.

When both sides are veneered and properly cured, saw to the interior dimensions of the rebated frame. This may not be a perfect square so check the diagonals as well, then rebate the panel to fit the frame. Check the depth of the rebate to achieve a flush surface. If the

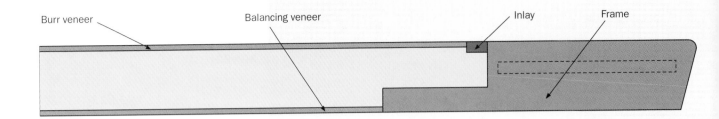

Burr veneer · Balancing veneer · Inlay · Frame

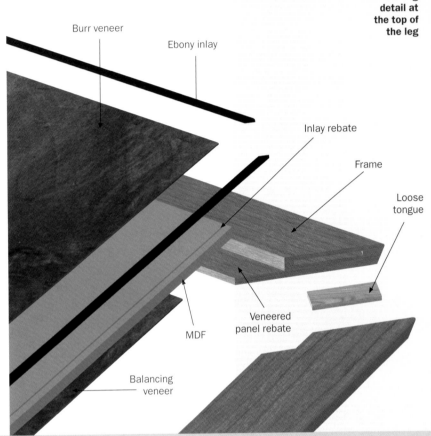

Burr veneer · Ebony inlay · Inlay rebate · Frame · Loose tongue · Veneered panel rebate · MDF · Balancing veneer

Fluting detail at the top of the leg

"After all, the appeal of a piece of work should rest on the plain truth stated by the grain and colour of the timber and by the line and form of the design, although a little help may sometimes be acceptable"

worst should happen, and the veneer panel drops below the surround, pack veneer on the rebate shelf to build up but this is a second best way of working! A strong, continuous glue line here is important for stability. Finally, rebate for the inlay, mitre and glue in place.

Legs

As for the legs, take the oversize blanks and thickness them on successive sides to remove a similar amount from each face. This minimises future bending whatever the environment the tables finish up in. Then, with the table saw set at 45°, remove successive corners to finish up with octagonal legs – make sure the faces are the same width! The design requires these faces to be converted to flutes and this is done on the spindle moulder or table router with a large diameter coving bit. There may

not be one big enough in the average workshop inventory so several passes with a smaller one maybe needed, finishing up with a suitable moulding plane or a piece of dowel with successive grit abrasive payer to get the fluting smooth and uniform. Depending on the finish obtained with the router, 100 grit will work quite fast but a proper finish can only be obtained with 240 grit, having gone conscientiously through 180 as well!

A feature to watch for at this stage is whether the legs are only a bit bent. This can result in a quite inadequate depth of cut on the router table because the concave side, resting on the table over the whole of its length, will lift the face being cut away from the cutter. This is one of the trickiest operations on this project and to minimise problems ensure the legs are straight!

With the outer shaping of the legs complete, select the inner corners and lay out for the mortices for the drawer box sides and back, the drawer top and bottom rails, and – at 45° to these – for the cross rails. The mortices for the sides and backs should be deep enough to allow for an internal mitre on the matching tenons. Also, because the leg is relatively slender, it's wise to form a double tenor here, with a shallow connecting groove. This work can be done with a plunge router, using a straight cutter about ⅓ the thickness of the sides and back. Finally, saw the legs to the required length and put a 3mm (⅛in) chamfer at the bottom, all round – this helps the table slide over carpet and helps to prevent splits if roughly moved.

David continues his project in the next article.

These tables were entered last year at the Axminster show and owe some inspiration to the winning pieces of Richard Williams in 1998

PHOTOGRAPHY BY ANTHONY BAILEY
ILLUSTRATIONS BY SIMON RODWAY

Sweet inspiration

David Applegate makes side tables in English walnut – part two

In the last article, David Applegate outlined his inspiration for the side tables in English walnut and how he set about the design and construction. In this second part, David completes the project.

Drawer box

Now machine the drawer box parts to thickness and width. Then, having selected which are to be the drawer fronts, rails and the sides and backs, saw to length. This must include the tenon lengths too.

Cut the shoulders of the corresponding tenons on the cross slide of the table saw. Don't cut the haunches on the saw – these will need to be curved to fit the fluted legs and must be left till later when each tenon is fitted to its matching mortice. The cheeks are cut on the table saw also, using a tall fence extension to ensure the parts being cut are at right angles to the blade. The edges of the tenons must be rounded to fit the mortices, although a bit of play is advisable to enable any slight mismatch to be rectified. Also, at this stage, machine a 3mm($1/8$in) groove along the top inside faces of the sides, back and top front rail to accommodate the tongue on the buttons which hold the table top on.

Undersides

The shaping of the undersides of the sides and backs of the carcass – and the lower drawer rail – should be left until just before assembly or, at the earliest, when all machining requiring parallelism of those parts has been completed. With so few pieces there's little point in employing the spindle moulder and making a cam for the cutter to follow – simply marking out by eye with a pencil, cutting on a bandsaw, finishing with a spokeshave and progressively finer grit paper was quite adequate. Symmetry is achieved by reversing the first one cut on the second, and splitting the shape difference! An ad hoc line, indeed!

The final addition to the shaping is a finely scratched line on the lower curves, done with a scratchstock. This is a piece of hacksaw blade, ground

Underside, showing split dust panel in order to achieve an easy fit

Top fixing and drawer runner

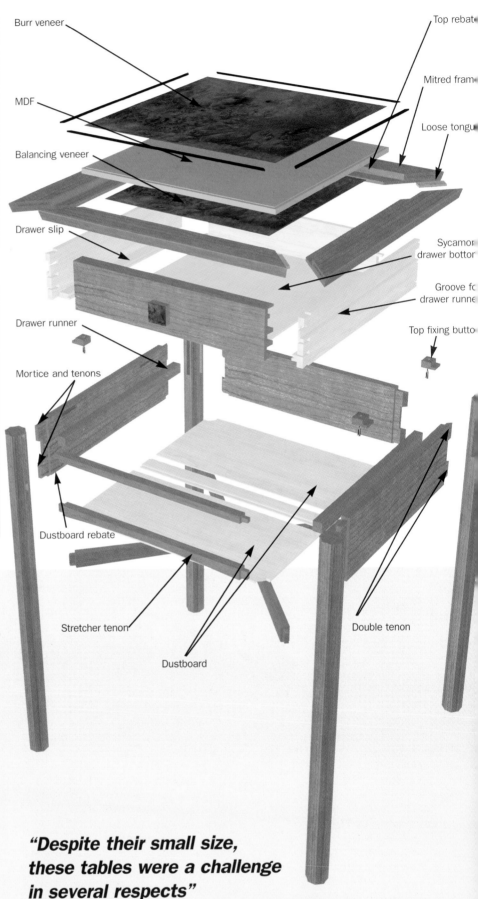

Burr veneer

Top rebate

MDF

Mitred frame

Balancing veneer

Loose tongue

Drawer slip

Sycamore drawer bottom

Groove for drawer runner

Drawer runner

Top fixing button

Mortice and tenons

Dustboard rebate

Stretcher tenon

Double tenon

Dustboard

to the shape required, and fitted in a comfortable holder. Using a scratchstock is like using a marking gauge except some wood has to be removed and this requires several strokes. Keep the blade at right angles to the work and remember that many light strokes will make better progress than a few heavy ones which may well dig in and tear the wood, rather than shape it.

All through the forming of the drawer box parts the datum has been their top inner surfaces. This is especially important when routing – or table sawing – for the oak drawer runners. It's essential these are level with each other so the drawer runs sweetly on them. Sand all surfaces with 180 and 240 grit paper – preferably Trimite.

Having completed this final work on the drawer box try a dry assembly, so wet assembly can be guaranteed a success. If all goes well, brush on to all the

"Despite their small size, these tables were a challenge in several respects"

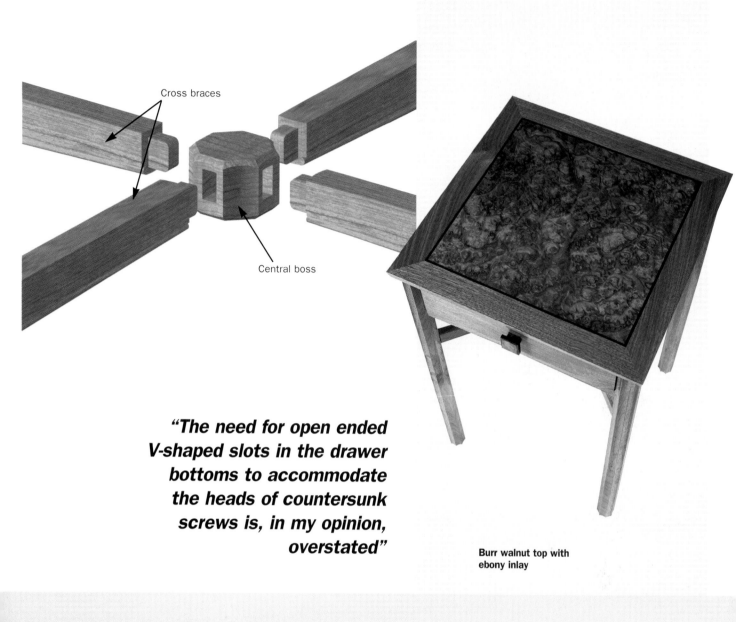

Cross braces

Central boss

"The need for open ended V-shaped slots in the drawer bottoms to accommodate the heads of countersunk screws is, in my opinion, overstated"

Burr walnut top with ebony inlay

surfaces not destined to be glued a coat of shellac sealer – I use Fiddes – and allow to dry. Sand with 320 grit but don't remove all the sanding dust as it forms a most effective parting agent for unwanted glue!

Gluing up

If all is satisfactory, gluing up is irreversible! Apply Cascamite to the side joints, ensuring the legs are parallel and out of winding. Be careful to remove the excess glue from the mortices receiving the back and drawer rails. Leave to set and then remove gently from the clamps. The spewed out glue can be carefully chipped off from the joint lines now thus proving the value of not wiping off the excess wet glue and removing the sanding dust! Then glue the back and drawer rails to the assembled sides – ensuring the legs are parallel and out of winding as before – and the drawer box is

square. Use the diagonals to check.

Cross-braces

The cross-braces are formed in a similar manner to the other tenoned parts. The central boss – an offcut from one of the legs – is too small to rout out safely unless, with much forethought, a shaped offcut about 150mm (6in) is available, so the mortices may have to be drilled out and finished with a chisel. Fitting the cross braces takes nerve and panache!

Clearly it's not possible to glue up at the same time as the earlier clampings. The rails have to be sprung in and, for this reason, the tenons may only be stubs – about half the length of those already glued. It's necessary to round off the corners of the tenons to get the required 'up and down' movement. A dry run is necessary here and it's satisfying to notice how the sub-assembly 'pings' into place. Be sure the rails are

perfectly aligned with each other. After gluing, light clamping will ensure a good appearance and, again, when dry, excess glue snaps off without any trouble!

Drawer

Having now achieved a satisfactory drawer box, the drawer needs to be made and fitted. Good quality work requires dovetails to both the front and back. These, preferably, should be hand-cut as it's not always possible to get the pins as fine using a router. The front was already selected and thicknessed with the drawer rails, so now fit the front precisely to fit the drawer aperture. A slight taper from front to back on all the fitted edges should permit the drawer front to enter about 5mm (3/16in) – not more!

Thickness the sycamore (*Acer pseudoplatanus*) drawer sides and back to 8mm (5/16in) then cut to length and width. Groove the sides to fit the oak drawer

"Handles are of primary importance to any piece of work"

Underside of drawer

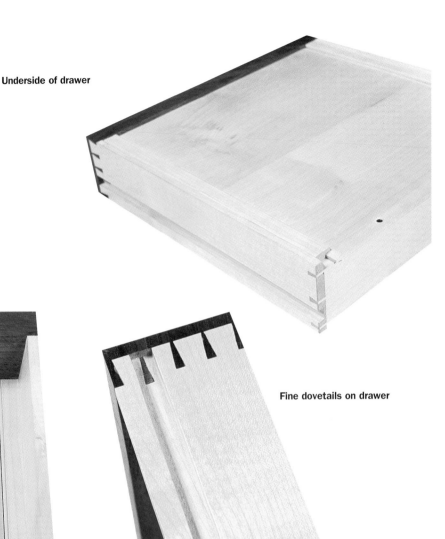

Drawer slip detail

Fine dovetails on drawer

runners using the top edge of the sides as the datum guide. The inner surface of the drawer front must be grooved to take the drawer bottom, while the back is reduced in width to allow the bottom to sit smoothly on its edge. Then, cut the dovetails in whatever time honoured way suits your preference – or your buyer! Sand the internal faces to remove pencil lines and plane marks, and coat with sanding sealer. Before gluing up, sand again with 320 grit Trimite. After applying, glue, clamp and ensure the groove in the drawer front is cleared out for the bottom to enter freely. Make absolutely certain the assembly is square and out of winding.

The drawer bottom, or floor, is 6mm (1/4in) thick sycamore; its sides relieved with a fluting cutter to 3mm (1/8in). It fits into two drawer slips grooved for the purpose and glued to the sides. These give a pleasant finished appear-

ance to a drawer as their length is equal to the distance between the drawer front and the back. For internal decorations, the slips have a groove scratched into them to match the groove on the box side members. Leave the assembly of the slips to the sides until after the drawer fits the carcass.

Table top and handles

The next major operation is to fit the table top. This is done by the use of 'buttons' which are screwed to the underside of the top, with the offset tongue located in the grooves in the sides and back and front rail. It's important the button tongue thickness matches the groove in the box members and, when screwed in position, it applies a slight clamping force between the top and box members. Sand the top to a uniform matt finishing with 320 grit.

With the table top in position, and the drawer fitted, the type and number of drawer handles needed can be decided upon. Handles are of primary importance to any piece of work. They're the first point of contact in everyday use and they alone answer the question, "how do I use this thing?" And, by definition, they must advertise their presence. Therefore, handles must be suited to the task in every way and the one on this project is a kind of model of the table top: a square of ebony (*Diospyrus sp*) with a piece of burr veneer planted on top. It's screwed in from the back of the drawer front and the hole for the screw head is filled with a walnut (*Juglans sp*) plug. Now the dustboard under the drawer can be made and fitted. This is a luxury and few tables of this kind I've seen have one. However, if it's good enough for a full chest of drawers it's good enough

"This project required a good deal of sanding of the components before the final finishing operations. It's essential to get rid of all the dust produced so wipe well..."

Fitting the drawer

To fit the drawer remove all excess glue and offer it up to the drawer box – where to plane off is apparent. Use a stout board clamped to the bench as wide as the internal length of the sides to give support while planing. Chamfer off the back end of the sides to facilitate planing from front to back. Use a sanding block when the drawer fits snugly over all its length, with 320 grit paper, and only to provide a good surface for a coat of sanding sealer.

When the drawer slides well in through the front aperture, test the fit of the oak runners on both the drawer sides and the carcass sides. Both should slide well without any rattle. Screw the runners to the carcass and obtain a good sliding fit of the drawer. Judicious use of scraper and sanding block may well be needed here. A scrape of wax polish helps to show 'high spots'. There is plenty more helpful advice to making a drawer and getting it to fit, which is beyond the scope of this article, so may I refer the reader to pages 148 and 149 of *Cabinetmaking – the Professional Approach* by Alan Peters.

The shellac sealer finish should also be applied to the drawer bottom. The slips are assembled to the drawer itself by sliding the slips and the bottom into the drawer while the glue between the slips and tire sides is still wet. Ensure no glue gets between the slips and the bottom. Chip off excess glue when the assembly is set and screw the bottom to the drawer back.

The need for open ended V-shaped slots in the drawer bottoms to accommodate the heads of countersunk screws is, in my opinion, overstated. It's easier, neater and simpler to insert the bottom into the drawer front, leaving about 3mm ($1/8$in) play and screwing the bottom to the back in that position. This arrangement permits the bottom to expand or contract into the drawer front. Finally, carefully plane off any excess thickness on the drawer slips so they become level with the sides.

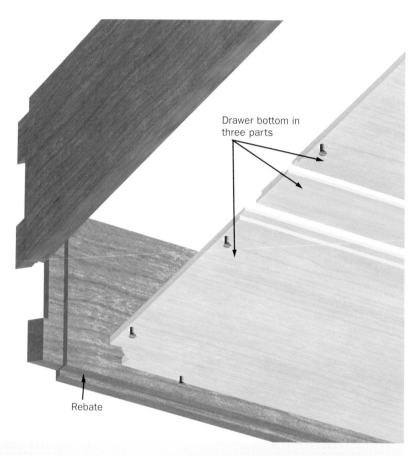

Drawer bottom in three parts

Rebate

for this project, as it finishes off the quality of construction.

It's necessary to fit this in three pieces, mainly because the cross-braces are in the way but also due to the fluted shapes of the legs. The dustboard parts sit on small batterns screwed to the lower edges of the carcass, held by No 2 woodscrews. It's important to ensure the centre piece overlaps the outer pieces, with a rebate on each, so movement can take place. The dustboard is finished to the same standard as the sycamore drawer parts.

Finishing

This project required a good deal of sanding of the components before the final finishing operations. It's essential to get rid of all the dust produced so wipe well – several times, if necessary – with clean 'lint free' cloths dampened with white spirit. The table top is finished with four coats of Rustin's Plastic Coating, cut back with 600 grit and 800 grit wet and dry, and white spirit; then finished with wax polish. The remainder of the project, drawer sides and bottoms included, is finished with Danish Oil – about four coats – de-nibbing with worn 320 grit paper, if necessary, followed by a wax polish.

Conclusion

Despite their small size, these tables were a challenge in several respects. The shaping of the legs; the fitting of the cross-braces; the veneering, and inlay of the top. The scratching of the shapes on the drawer box parts and the cross braces was also problematic but the final effect of seeing two identical tables, rich in their polished walnut and offset by the accompanying furniture, was almost as much reward as their final sale.

Cabinetmaking – the Professional Approach
by Alan Peters
Published by Stobart & Sons
Out of print

Thalia's table

MAIN ILLUSTRATION BY IAN HALL

● **SCOTT WOYKA**
is a fifth-
generation
woodworker.
Although he
trained as an
aeronautic
engineer, he could
not resist
returning to
work with wood.
He has been
running a
workshop for
four years in the
harbour town of
Falmouth in
Cornwall and
produces
furniture to
commission,
mostly to his own
designs.

ABOVE RIGHT:
Curves are the
theme for this
writing table

**RIGHT: Soft
shaping takes
away the sharp
edges found on
traditional
writing desks**

Scott Woyka makes curves his theme

MY MUSE for this table was my girlfriend, whose shapely curves I used as an inspiration for the legs. I named the piece after Thalia, one of the three graces. It was to be an exhibition piece, and so I kept the wood in the workshop for several months before starting on the making. I was not sure how the 110mm (4in) sycamore (*Acer pseudoplatanus*) would cope with being brought into the dryness of the workshop, but it has remained very stable.

Timber selection
Sycamore varies in tone from quite a bright white to a beigy-white, grey, or yellow – the brightest white being preferable.

Care should be taking to select wood from the same board for use in the same parts of the piece – for instance, the frames should be made from one board, whilst the legs can be

made from another.

Sycamore has the most fantastic lustre which is like the nap of velvet, so parts must be orientated to give the same reflection of light.

Construction
Four frames are made up for the rails. The back and side rails could be made from solid wood –140 by 20mm (5½ by ¾in) – but I chose to make them as frame-and-panel to reduce any movement, and to add a little detail.

The front receives the drawers. These rail frames are bare-face tenoned into the legs – the shoulder of the tenon being curved to meet the leg.

Legs
First, the legs are machined square and to size – 96 by 96 by 744mm (3¾ by 3¾ by 29¼in) and 12mm (½in) mortices are cut to receive the rails. Not having a morticer, I did this by hand, first removing the

waste in the drill press, then chopping out with a chisel. The inside faces of the mortices must be really neat, as the tenons are bare-faced – so sharpen up your chisel!

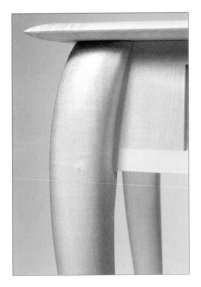

The outline of the leg is based on various radii. I made the curves fairly subtle as they would be exaggerated when cut in two planes. A template is made from 6mm (¼in) ply and this is drawn on the face and side of each leg.

The top part of the curve, on the inside of each leg, needs to be made accurately as it is met by the shoulder of each frame tenon. It could be done on the bandsaw and shaved to the line, but I chose to do it with my router trammel. The trammel is made from 8mm (⅝in) steel rod and a small steel plate welded together.

Curves

Use a piece of 18mm (¾in) MDF as a base. Mark out the centre of the radius for the curves, and the relevant position for the legs. Screw on a block of wood 96mm (3¾in) thick with an 8mm (⅝in) hole at the centre of the radius. Also screw down blocks of wood in appropriate positions to hold the legs in place, using wedges to keep them tight.

Using a 6mm (¼in) straight router bit, rout this curve up to 10mm (⅜in) deep on two faces. In one plane this can be done on the inside face, and in the other it has to be done on the outside face – otherwise, you would remove this work when sawing off the waste.

When this is done, saw off the waste close to the routed line – you can then flush-trim this sawn line, running the router from above with a top bearing bit down to half the thickness. Then, with the router in a router table, use a 50mm (2in) bottom bearing flush trim bit to remove the rest.

Remove the remaining waste on the bandsaw, sawing to the template line. On the top portion of the leg, saw down the line as far as you can without removing it entirely, as these square faces are used for clamping in the glue-up. To saw on the second plane, the waste is glued back on with hot melt glue to give a flat face to sit on the saw table.

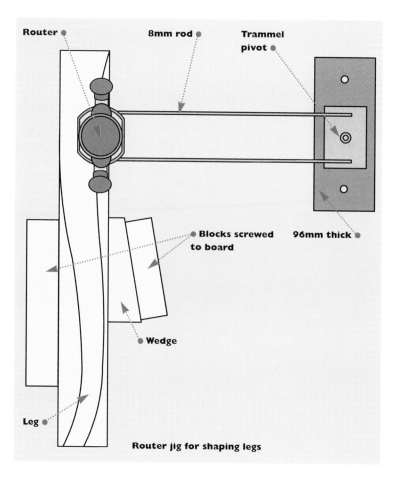

Router jig for shaping legs

Router •   8mm rod •   Trammel pivot •

Blocks screwed to board   96mm thick

Wedge

Leg •

RIGHT: Internal
construction
detail of side
panels – note
button holding
top

FAR RIGHT:
Drawer runners
and drawer stop
detail

Shaping

Before you start the shaping, cut several holes in 6mm (¼in) ply from a 30mm, (1³⁄₁₆in) to say a 73mm, (2⅞in) diameter. Mark the leg at the various heights where its width matches that of a hole. As you are shaping, these can be slipped over the end to see where timber removal is necessary.

To hold the leg whilst shaping, use any means possible – a sash cramp held in the vice will hold it at each end, or 150mm (6in) G-clamps will hold it on the bench top with cork or rubber blocks to cushion it. Most of the shaping is done with a spokeshave, followed by a cabinet scraper and sandpaper.

RIGHT: Leg
template

BELOW: Sequence
for cutting and
shaping legs

Frames and panels

Next, the four frames are made up from 20mm (¾in) timber, with mortice and tenon construction, using 8mm (⁵⁄₁₆in) mortices. The panels are machined to 14mm (⁹⁄₁₆in) thick. The mouldings are applied first with a straight cutter,

followed by a 10mm (⅜in) radius cutter in the router table, running the work against a fence. A one-piece panel mould cutter, of whatever profile suits you, would achieve this more quickly, and requires less cleaning up.

The groove for the panels is cut in the frames so that the panels will sit just shy of the frame surface. This is done with a groover to 8mm (⁵⁄₁₆in) deep – you will have to square up the ends of the grooves on the horizontal pieces where they do not run through. These are then glued-up. The next day they can be cleaned up ready to cut the tenons – this is done using the router trammel again to form the curved shoulder. First, check the depth to rout down to by using some scrap of the same thickness and test it in the mortices.

The tenons are then mitred to length, and the top and bottom shoulders cut and trimmed to the curve of the leg. Check each one for fit.

Drawer runners

The drawer runners are machined to 40 by 35mm (1⁹⁄₁₆ by 1⅜in) square and a 15 by 15mm (¹⁹⁄₃₂ by ¹⁹⁄₃₂in) rebate is taken out. The kickers are 40 by 25mm (1⁹⁄₁₆ by 1in) – these are all morticed into the front and back frames.

Glue-up

After sanding all the components down to 240 grit, do a dry run, trying to contain your excitement as the piece takes shape. First, the main carcass, consisting of front and back frames and the runners and kickers, is glued-up and left overnight.

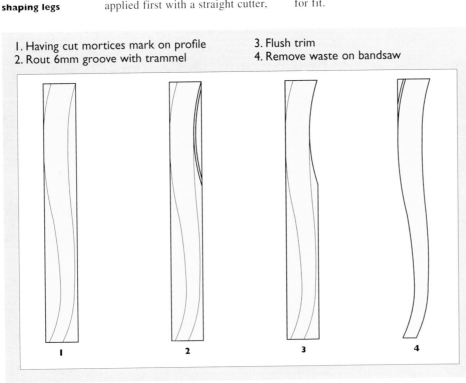

1. Having cut mortices mark on profile
2. Rout 6mm groove with trammel
3. Flush trim
4. Remove waste on bandsaw

1   2   3   4

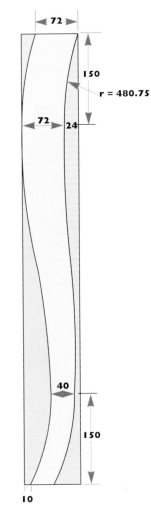

72

150

r = 480.75

72   24

40

150

10

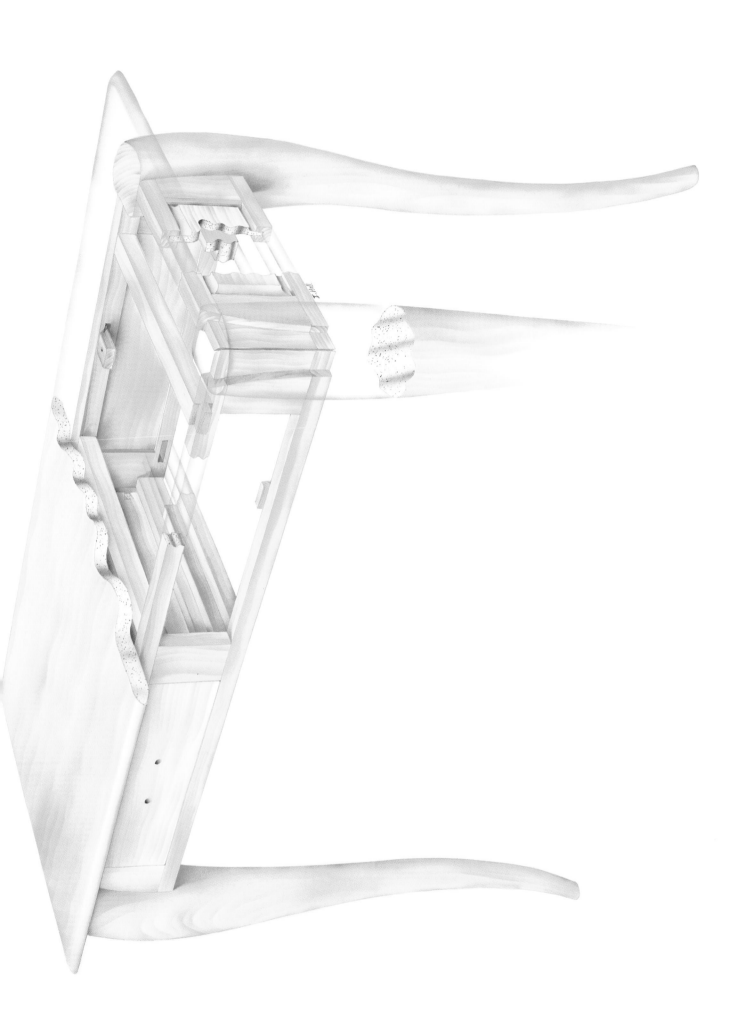

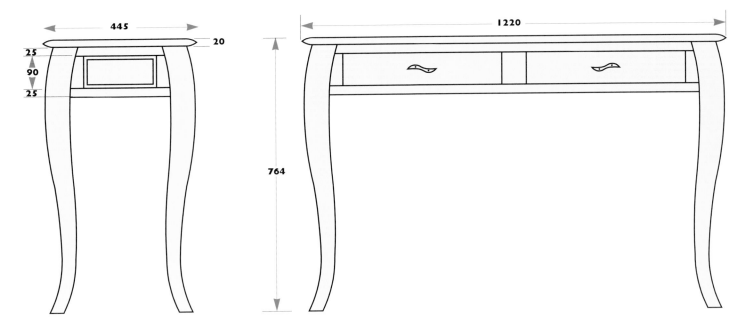

DRAWERS

All the timber for the drawers is quarter sawn. The 10mm (3/8in) thick sides are lap dovetailed to the fronts. The backs are housed into the sides – all are grooved to receive 6mm (1/4in) sycamore-veneered ply at the bottom.

The fronts must be drilled for the handles before glue-up using a 4mm drill

Drawer dovetails

(1/8in) and 12mm (1/2in) drill to recess the nuts. A 2mm (1/16in) chamfer was put on the drawer fronts and on the drawer openings in the frames to attract the eye.

Small pieces of sycamore, 40 by 20 by 6mm (1 9/16 by 3/4 by 1/4in), are screwed to the back of the front frame as drawer-stops. They also stop the drawer coming out completely as the drawer back is the full depth of the drawer. I am sure I am not the only one to have pulled a drawer out fully – only to watch the contents spill to the floor.

For the next glue-up you must assemble each end pair of legs with their panel, and glue these to the main carcass.

Clamp-up by putting two clamps across each end pair of legs and one across the front and back – when ready, remove the clamps and clean up, ensuring that the top surface is flush.

The top part of the leg can now be shaped as before, using any means available to hold the table down. I used a bench holdfast and various pieces of wood to lever pressure onto the table.

Top

Slots are routed at this stage for the buttons – three along the front and the back, and one at each end – for this, use a 10mm (3/8in) groover. The router base can rest on the kickers, the frame tops, and the top of the legs – so you should have no trouble with balancing. Of course a more organised craftsman might wish to do these before glue-up!

The buttons are cut on the bandsaw from 20 by 25mm (3/4 by 1in) stock and checked for a tight fit in the grooves.

For the top, I had some lovely 50mm (2in) stock which I bookmatched and finished to 20mm (3/8in). The edge mould is semi-elliptical and is done on the router table in two cuts – although it can easily be achieved with a hand plane, checking against a template.

Finishing

Thalia's table was sprayed with two coats of cellulose sanding sealer, before having a wax polish applied.

Conclusion

If you have managed to get this far, you will have a very versatile piece of furniture – a table of this type can be used in almost any room in the house and serve a number of different purposes. Using sycamore alone was a deliberate choice as I did not want to distract from the form, but I would love to make this piece again using a second wood for the legs, drawer fronts panels, and top. One improvement I might make would be the drawer bottoms – whilst using ply means that you can save on both time and materials, you can't beat the real stuff.

HANDLES

Having not really worked with metal before, making the handles was quite a refreshing task. Being homogeneous, metal is really easy to shape, with no grain to complicate matters.

Take two pieces of 50 by 12 by 150mm (2 by 7/16 by 6in) brass stock. Mark the positions

The flowing handles continue the theme of curves

for the supports at 75mm (3in) apart, and then drill and tap with a 2BA thread. The brass rod is then threaded with a 2BA dye to give 4 lengths of 40mm (1 9/16in).

I machined the supports on a metal lathe with fairly limited tooling and cleaned up with some emery cloth – the brass washers were also turned on the lathe.

The handles are cut to shape on the bandsaw, then filed and sanded to shape. Both handles and supports are polished up on a polishing wheel. The brass can be lacquered, but they say this can flake, so I chose to leave them bare. The occasional wipe with some Brasso will bring them up beautifully.

Table for two

Ian Saville makes a duet music table

PHOTOGRAPHY BY ANTHONY BAILEY
ILLUSTRATIONS BY SIMON RODWAY

With the drawers open the table's discreet function is revealed

Having originally been a geologist, Ian Saville re-trained as a furniture-maker in Sheffield. He set up his present workshop in Derbyshire in 1993 where he specialises in making furniture for musicians

A speciality of our workshop is furniture for musicians and, with the deadline for the exhibition 'Musical Connections' at the Ruskin Gallery in Sheffield approaching, I needed to produce a couple of exhibition pieces to complement the items that we produce in small batches. Time was short, as seems to be the case with speculative

"I wanted it to be as delicate as possible, whilst retaining adequate strength, in order to complement the instruments to be played at it"

pieces where remuneration is rarely immediate, so they needed to be fairly straightforward to make, whilst retaining integrity.

Duet table

I intended one of the pieces to be a table that incorporated a pair of desks at which duets could be played. I wanted it to be as delicate as possible, whilst retaining adequate strength, in order to complement the instruments to be played at it.

Materials

As for the materials, it seemed appropriate to use ripple sycamore in part of the table. I had a small quantity of veneer in stock, which I decided to use for the main area of the top, and also some finely rippled solid material,

gleaned from a violin-maker who was to exhibit with me, to make the drawers and desks. For the main structure of the table English cherry (*Prunus avium*) was chosen both to complement and mildly contrast with the sycamore (*Acer pseudoplatanus*) – I also happened to have some suitable, lightly rippled material in stock!

Design

The design for the table was arrived at quite quickly, partly out of necessity, but also because I liked the idea of the legs being prominent and cradling the top. The use of gentle curves throughout the piece gives it a restful look.

Cutting

The components are all cut out from the same piece of 50mm (2in) cherry and, after a period to allow the pieces to settle down, they are planed to size.

Size

The size of the desk is governed by the size of sheet music but was made to the smallest dimensions practical. The size of the desk therefore determines the overall size of the table, which I wanted to be as compact as possible. Similarly the height of the drawer, just enough to contain the desk, stay and serrated rails, governs the width of the table side rails. The overall look of the table is, I think, very pleasing whilst being robust enough to cope with its intended light and careful use.

RIGHT: **Table with drawers closed – a simple and elegant design**

Subtle drawer handle

The legs are initially left square in section to allow for morticing.

Morticing

The mortices for the side rails are cut first, the rails having large shoulders to allow for the rebates to be cut in them. They are cut so that the rails are flush with the inside face of the legs, allowing the rails to also form the drawer guides.

The mortices for the drawer rails are then cut and are able to pass over the side rail mortices giving greater strength. The mortices for the central cross rail are also cut in the side rails.

Side rails

The side rails are then rebated top and bottom and tenoned. The 10mm (⅜in) deep by 15mm (⅝in) wide rebates enable the drawer runners and kickers to be located easily after assembly of the piece and give a positive location. Care must be taken to ensure the rebates are parallel to give a constant depth to the drawer housing.

Drawer rails

The drawer rails protrude only 20mm (¾in) across the leg to allow the drawer fronts to be inset between the legs, and are tenoned into them with a short

The drop-in top is a fine piece of book-matched ripple sycamore veneers

tenon. The back of the rail sits in the rebate in the side rails and may be pegged or screwed into this after assembly.

The top drawer rail is only 10mm (⅜in) thick but that is considered to be adequately thick, especially after the veneered top is fixed down. The bottom drawer rail is 15mm (⅝in) thick for greater strength, and a curved rail is added underneath to provide greater rigidity. The 15mm (⅝in) runners set in a 10mm (⅜in) rebate produce a small

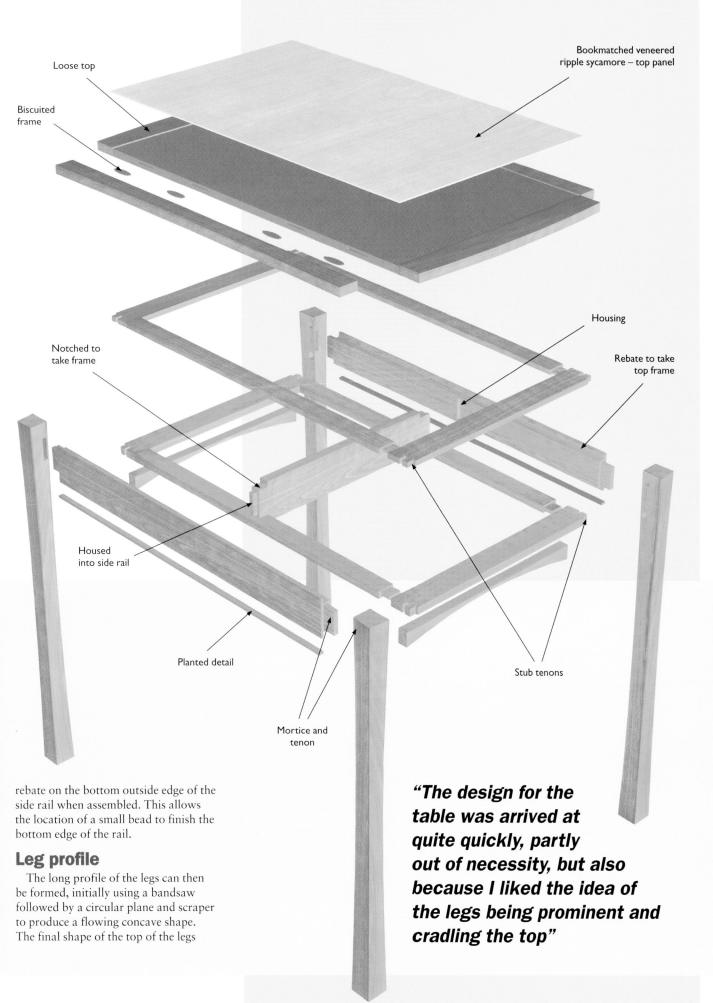

Loose top

Bookmatched veneered
ripple sycamore – top panel

Biscuited
frame

Notched to
take frame

Housing

Rebate to take
top frame

Housed
into side rail

Stub tenons

Planted detail

Mortice and
tenon

rebate on the bottom outside edge of the
side rail when assembled. This allows
the location of a small bead to finish the
bottom edge of the rail.

Leg profile

The long profile of the legs can then
be formed, initially using a bandsaw
followed by a circular plane and scraper
to produce a flowing concave shape.
The final shape of the top of the legs

*"The design for the
table was arrived at
quite quickly, partly
out of necessity, but also
because I liked the idea of
the legs being prominent and
cradling the top"*

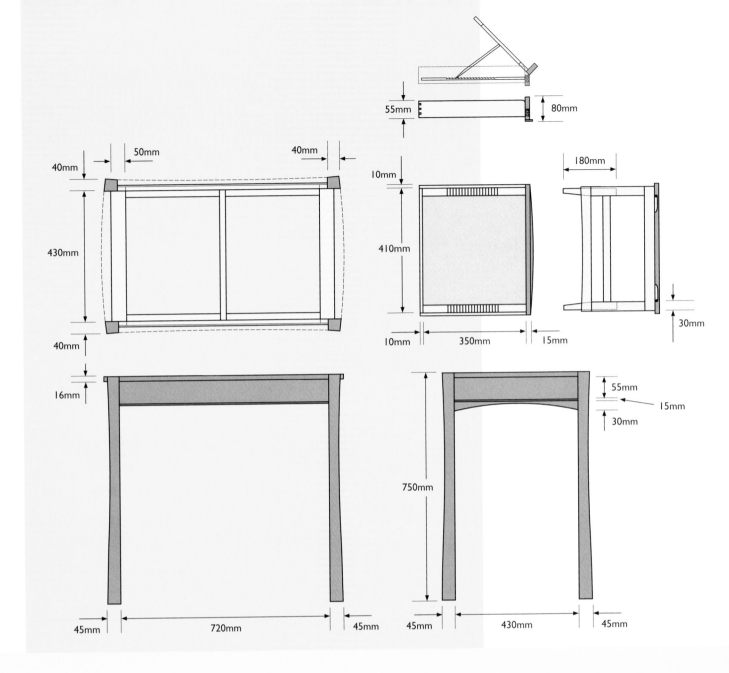

is left until after the veneered top has been made.

Assembly

After cleaning and sanding the surfaces to 360 grit, the table frame can be assembled. The side rails are first

The desk neatly folds away in the drawer

glued into the legs and allowed to dry. The drawer rails and central rails are then glued in. Suitably shaped cramping blocks must be made to protect the legs when cramping and a careful check must be made for squareness and wind.

The drawer rails and kickers can now be fitted into the rebates, the ends being stub tenoned into the drawer rails and having a half lap joint over the notch in the central rail. The rails and kickers are screwed into the rebate and plugged.

Top

The next step is to make the top. The book-matched and carefully jointed sycamore is first taped together and then glued to the substrate of 15mm (5/8in) MDF. The pressing can be successfully achieved using cauls and cramps, but in this case it was done using a handy veneer press. A balancing veneer is glued to the underside to prevent distortion of

the top. After pressing, the slightly oversize top should be carefully cut and planed so as to fit exactly between the inside corners of the protruding legs of the table frame.

Edge lipping

The top is then edged with slightly oversized lippings of cherry, these being attached using biscuits for strength and location. The lippings are cut to the exact length of the veneered top so as to form a notch at the corners to fit around the legs. The top and bottom surfaces of the lippings can then be carefully hand-planed flush with the surface of the veneer.

The top is then fitted to the table, and the side and end curves marked out on both the lippings and the tops of the legs. The curves can then be cut using bandsaw and circular plane and the legs flared into the curve by careful use of

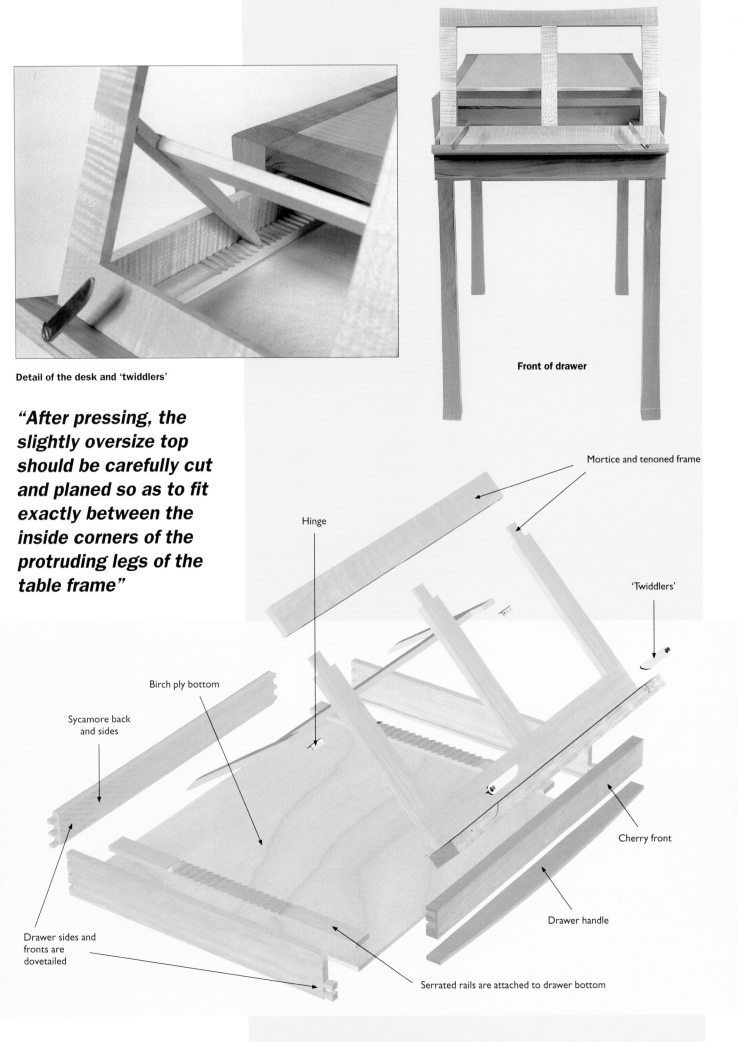

Detail of the desk and 'twiddlers'

Front of drawer

"After pressing, the slightly oversize top should be carefully cut and planed so as to fit exactly between the inside corners of the protruding legs of the table frame"

Mortice and tenoned frame

Hinge

'Twiddlers'

Sycamore back and sides

Birch ply bottom

Cherry front

Drawer handle

Drawer sides and fronts are dovetailed

Serrated rails are attached to drawer bottom

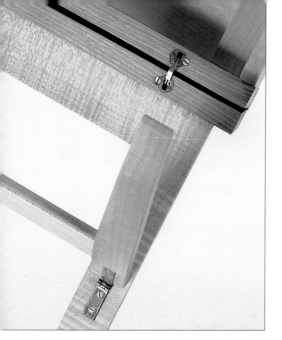

Fine soss hinges in the folding drawer front and the hinged stay

Desks

The desks themselves are made up using 10mm (3/8in) thick strips of ripple sycamore tenoned together to form a separate frame. The stay for the desk is made from material of similar dimensions, the supports being tapered before assembly of the cross rail. The top of the desk is curved to echo the curve of the table top ends. The desks can then be attached to the drawer front tops, using small biscuits, to form the rest for the music.

The serrated rails to hold the supports are made initially as a single wide piece, the grooves being cut square over a table saw and then angled by hand. The piece is then cut down the middle to provide two identical rails which are screwed to the sides of the drawer base. The page retainers – or 'twiddlers' – are cut from brass sheet and secured in shaped rebates by brass screws.

As the drawer has to be pulled a long way out before the desk can be raised, small rotating stops are added to the backs of the top drawer rails to prevent the drawer from being accidentally fully withdrawn.

Underside of the drawer front is scalloped for a hand-hold

Axminster winner

Ian Saville entered this delightful piece into the 1998 F&C competition at Axminster and won a well-deserved 3rd prize in the Professional category. It demonstrates all the criteria of rightness of design, fitness for purpose, superb execution and an almost faultless finish, that the judges were looking for.

With over 40 entries in the Professional category, all of which were of a particularly high standard, the judges had to be very discerning indeed in making their choices – and didn't find it an easy job!

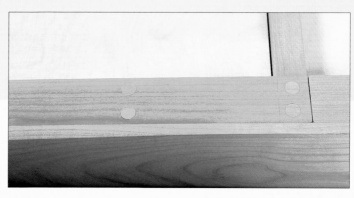

Under-frame is screwed and plugged into side rail rebates

hand-plane and scraper. The top is attached by screws through the runners, the screws being well countersunk to prevent fouling the drawers. The tops of the legs can now be carefully planed flush with the table surface.

Drawers

The drawers are constructed and fitted traditionally, except for the drawer fronts, using 10mm (⅜in) thick sycamore for the sides and backs. Birch plywood is used for the drawer bottoms because the serrated rails for the desk supports are attached to them – solid wood drawer bottoms would not be able to move with these rails attached.

Drawer fronts

The drawer fronts are made from a single piece of cherry each. The pieces

are bandsawn along their length so as to provide a fixed base and a hinged top piece, which also forms the rest for the music desk. The base piece is dovetailed to the sides of the drawer and under-hangs the drawer sides. This provides a drawer stop against the bottom drawer rail and, with the addition of a beading strip underneath, allows the placing of a hidden finger pull under the drawer front.

Hinges

The top pieces of the drawer fronts are then hinged to the bases. I was initially going to use butt hinges for this

but they would have spoilt the clean appearance of the closed drawers. A search through a relevant catalogue resulted in some tiny soss hinges being ordered. Although initially sceptical as to the quality of these hinges, on arrival they were found to be small but perfectly formed and can be installed, with some care, to provide a perfect solution.

Finishing

Final cleaning and sanding to 400 grit, and softening of arrises, is followed by several thin applications of Danish oil, and then a light waxing.

Tables with extensions can be useful allies in modern houses which are spatially challenged

PHOTOGRAPHY BY
ANTHONY BAILEY
ILLUSTRATIONS BY
SIMON RODWAY

David Kortright retired from the Metropolitan Police five years ago and attended a course in fine cabinetmaking in Devon. Since then he has been making furniture at his workshop in Surrey, concentrating on commission work

David Kortright designs and makes a round dining table with eight extension sections

Expansion in the round

My client said "I want a round table to seat six that expands to a round table to seat eight." "Sorry," I replied, "can't be done."

Twenty four hours later I was eating humble pie and telling her that the piece could be made.

"Then do it." she said. So I did.

Ernest Joyce lays out standard dimensions for tables and chairs; a round six-seater comes out at 1200mm (3ft 9 1/4in) diameter, an eight-seater at 1600mm (5ft 3in) – the table surface being about 765mm (2ft 6in) above the ground. These are useful guides, but it

would be wrong to follow them slavishly as other factors, such as chair seat height and the size of the customer, must have some bearing.

Design

My design process starts with scrap paper and doodles. I had already been to see the room where the table was to be located, and discussed the decoration and other furnishings. I receive inspiration in small bits and develop it slowly, then, when I am sure of my direction, switch the scrap paper for my sketch book and draw the parts I like –

perhaps a veneer pattern or a curved shape for the pedestal.

Then I start to blend them together – when the sketch begins to look like a table I move to a sheet of birch (*betula sp*) ply and draw full-size.

Usually at this stage I would start to build, but a table that is all curves needs looking at more closely, so in this case I built a model at 5:1 scale glued together with hot melt glue. As the design incorporated the use of extensions, I needed to prove that the system for supporting them worked. I planned to have a 200mm (7⅞in) rim, divided into eight pieces slotting around the small table, each piece to be supported on both sides.

The original idea was to have wooden sliders housed under the table that would pull out and support each piece. A full-sized mock-up demonstrated the lack of enough support, for it allowed the extension piece to drop when weight was applied. When any attempt was made to make the housing more rigid by

"A full-sized mock-up demonstrated the lack of enough support, for it allowed the extension piece to drop when weight was applied"

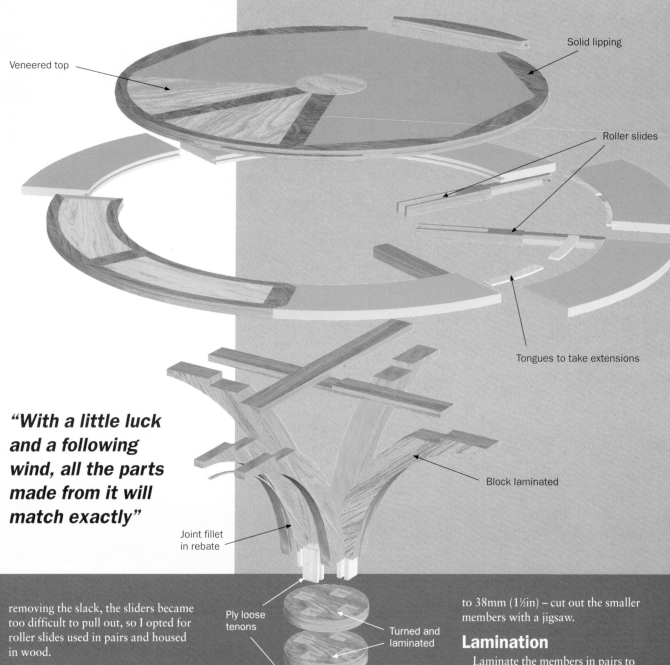

Veneered top

Solid lipping

Roller slides

Tongues to take extensions

Block laminated

"With a little luck and a following wind, all the parts made from it will match exactly"

Joint fillet
in rebate

Ply loose
tenons

Turned and
laminated

Solid feet

Pedestal
support

Half lap

removing the slack, the sliders became too difficult to pull out, so I opted for roller slides used in pairs and housed in wood.

Pedestal

The full-sized drawing is enlisted for the production of two master templates of the main curved pedestal members. This template is carefully made in 6mm (¼in) ply to the exact size required – with a little luck and a following wind, all the parts made from it will match exactly.

The templates are also used for the construction of four jigs, one for each curve and two curves on each member. Employing the template as a stencil, draw out eight shapes of each member from 5mm (2in) oak (*Quercus robur*) – each member will require two pieces of oak. The smaller bottom members are cut from one piece of wood. The larger pieces can be cut out from the rough timber with a jigsaw. Use the planer thicknesser to reduce all

to 38mm (1½in) – cut out the smaller members with a jigsaw.

Lamination

Laminate the members in pairs to produce 76mm (3in) thickness, and clamp up tight with Titebond. When the glue is set, stencil the exact shape on the template and cut on the bandsaw to within 5mm (³⁄₁₆in) of this line.

Each laminated piece is then mounted on the first jig. The spindle moulder is set with a straight cutter and a ring fence, and any wood that protrudes beyond the jig is spindled off. In the absence of a spindle moulder, this part could be done with a circular plane – more precision with the bandsaw pays off if a plane is employed. Use a new 6TPI blade and cut up to, but not over, the line.

Doughnut

The doughnut is made from two pieces of 250 by 250 by 38mm (10 by 10 by 1½in) timber planed, thicknessed and laminated as above.

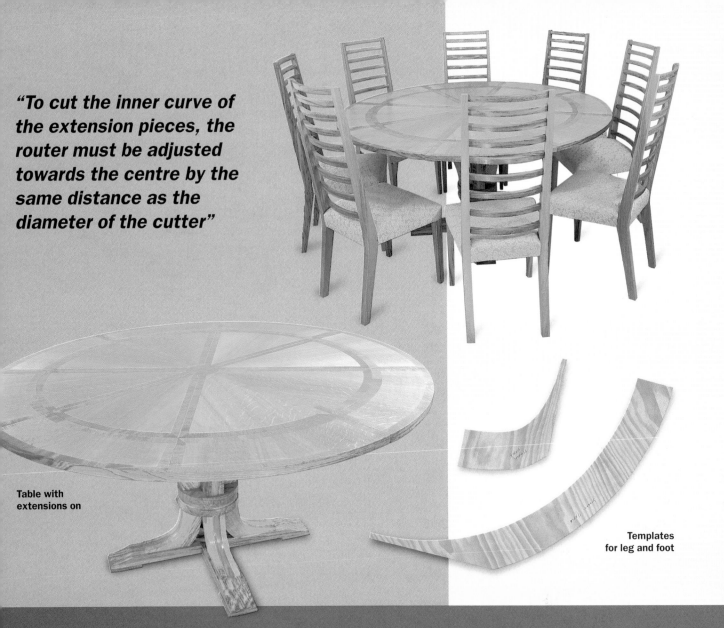

"To cut the inner curve of the extension pieces, the router must be adjusted towards the centre by the same distance as the diameter of the cutter"

Table with extensions on

Templates for leg and foot

A compass is employed to scribe a 250mm (10in) disc which is bandsawn and screwed to the lathe faceplate with a piece of 12mm (½in) sacrificial MDF between the wood and the metal faceplate.

The disc is turned to an outside diameter of 250mm (10in) and a 75mm (3in) hole turned.

The lamination of the main members is hidden by a 3mm (⅛in) trench filled in with a curved moulding.

Top

The top is made from 25mm MDF to enable veneer to be arranged in pattern. MDF remains stable – unlike timber for which a 1% allowance for movement must be allowed – meaning 12mm (½in) of movement for my 1200mm (3ft 9¼in) table – enough to cause mayhem, chaos and tragedy.

A solid lipping is required to prevent MDF showing around the edge. Each piece is butted and biscuited to the disc. A similar operation is executed on eight

small pieces of MDF destined for the extension pieces. The cutting of the disc, first in the MDF and again after the lipping is fitted, is a job for the incredible router – an ingenious device called a router trammel is made and anchored at the centre of the board, the router being pulled round to create a perfect circle.

Cut a shallow 1mm (½in) trench first, then cut the waste away with a jigsaw as close to the line as possible. Bring the router back to true the edge, taking about 5mm (3/16in) depth on each pass. The bigger the router bit the better – spiral bits may be worth a try.

Inner curve

To cut the inner curve of the extension pieces, the router must be adjusted towards the centre by the same distance as the diameter of the cutter. The cutting of the outside diameter is left until after the extension pieces have been fitted.

A groove now has to be cut in the edge of the table to accept the lips on the

extension pieces – the router must be adjusted towards the centre by the same distance as the diameter of the cutter. I used a slotting cutter, mounting the router on a piece of 9mm (3/8in) ply so that it could be held firmly, flat on the table surface with the cutter hanging down. This is a dicey operation – and dust extraction is a joke here – so a face mask is called for. I have the feeling that I will be told that this is unacceptable practice and await comments with interest as I could not think of another way to do it!

Veneering

The top comprises an arrangement of eight segments, each having an oak veneer centrepiece surrounded by a brown oak veneer border. All the corners are mitred and the grain of the border is short. Each segment is separated from the next by 3mm (⅛in) boxwood (*Buxus sp*) stringing. The extensions are a continuation of the segment, with a brown oak border all

High-tech from scrap

The scalpel trammel is a high tech piece of sophisticated tooling. It consists of a suitable length of scrap wood with a nail hammered into one end and a thin kerf cut at a precise distance from the nail into which a scalpel blade is pushed.

Solid top

Rolle
slides

Solid sides

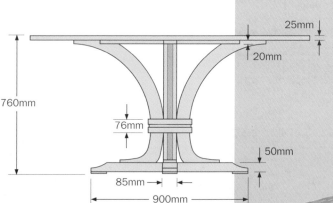

round. Cut the side borders first, oversize, and true one edge. Prepare a strip of veneer for the curved borders and cut it into pieces approximately 50mm (2in) long. Cut a thin wedge from each and glue it up again into a curved, segmented form.

Tape the segmented curve and, using the scalpel trammel, cut the two curves into it. A centre point is marked on a piece of scrap board, and the trammel used to mark the outline of the border piece.

Light cuts

The segmented veneer is then taped over the markings and cut with the trammel using several light cuts. The same process is carried through the rest of the veneering until all the pieces are made. The mitres in the veneer can be cut with a scalpel.

Fit the border pieces over-length so that adjacent pieces overlap one another. Then mark the mitre by measurement and cut the mitre from

the back, with the face side of the veneer on the cutting board to obtain a tight join.

Having cut all the pieces to size, join them together with little strips of masking tape stretched across the join. Finish the side by running the tape down the length of the join. On the other side of the veneer bend the join open, run a thin line of glue into the join, close it up and run another long strip of tape down the join.

When the glue has set, carefully remove all the tape – the veneer will hold together if treated with respect, and can

be pressed without the problem of trying to remove tape that has been under pressure.

Pressing task

The table top and extensions are then prepared to take adhesives – I have my own theories on this. The surface must be flat and clean. MDF is likely to have collected all sorts of impurities in manufacture and handling. Remove these with 180 grit in a half-sheet orbital sander, taking off dirt, pencil marks, or specs of glue on the surface prior to veneering.

With veneers cut and surface prepared, it is time to press. My ➤

Sticky conundrum

I have read several books and articles that say the surface should be keyed with a toothing plane or coarse abrasive to enable the glue to grip. This is not my understanding of the nature of adhesive at all. Adhesive is made up of large, long molecules. Molecules will bind together if held close enough – normally it is not possible to hold two items together close enough for the molecules to bind, but the long molecules of the adhesive form a bridge which binds them together. Keying or scratching will only hold the parts further away from each other. Furthermore, if glue needs a key to hold onto, why will it not hold end-grain, on which there are lots of places to grip?

Pump on the cheap

For this job I had to get a new vacuum bag, mine being too small. Pumps are expensive, but if the parts are obtained separately the final bill can be significantly cheaper than buying the kit. I seal the bag with two batons and three clamps and have no problem with this method at all.

LEFT **Router trammel for cutting true circle on top**

RIGHT **Underneath showing runners**

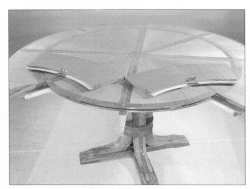
LEFT **Extension pieces and runners**

RIGHT **Runner in use**

➤ workshop is too small for a veneer press – I've even seen presses that I could put my workshop into! This means an alternative method must be found.

I've tried hammer veneering with hide glue and with Titebond, but the heat tends to shrink the veneer and could result in unwanted gaps in a complicated pattern. That leaves the vacuum press – a PVC bag and a vacuum pump.

The first trick of vacuum veneering is to ensure that the bag does not seal itself as it pumps the air out, so losing its vacuum – grooves in one of the cauls provide air passages. To avoid unwelcome surprises place the veneers, cauls etc. in the bag and seal it dry. When satisfied, apply the glue, stick the veneers top and bottom, press and pray.

Fitting runners

When the perfect table top comes out of the bag, trim the overlapping veneer with a router fitted with a straight bearing cutter. The balancing veneer on the underside is sanded and finished, in this case with pre-catalysed lacquer. Steel roller bearing runners, commonly found in pairs on drawers, are fitted. This method ensures the runner will pull easily, with almost no drop, providing ample support for the extension lippings.

Also fitted are the circular catches which hold the extension pieces in place. The un-extended table has a groove all round its rim to accept the extension pieces, but an empty groove is not aesthetically pleasing. I made up some 6mm thick mouldings to fit into the groove which improved the appearance enormously.

Finishing

The table top can then be turned over and the top sanded and finished. Pre-catalysed lacquer is made to be sprayed but it can be applied with a fine-haired – expensive – brush.

The lacquer, thinned 50/50 with thinners, is applied generously and left to dry. The fumes coming off when doing this are awful – if a face mask and appropriate filter is available, ensure the operation is carried out outside on a dry, warm, windless day. Do not on any account try this indoors without protection.

Apply three coats, sanding each with 240 grit and finishing the last coat with light grey Webrax 1200 on a random orbit sander. To achieve the desired sheen I finished with wax applied with 0000 wire wool.

The finished top is fastened to the pedestal using inset nuts in the underside of the top and 'T' bolts through the upper pedestal curves. This makes the table easy to 'knock down' and transport. My trusting client had arranged a mammoth dinner party on the evening of the delivery day – and I'm happy to report that there were no hitches. ■

Small-scale dining

Richard Jones makes
a modest dining table

Richard Jones trained as a cabinetmaker and, after some years as a craftsman with furniture workshops, spent nine years teaching MA students of Furniture Design & Craft at Heriot Watt University in Edinburgh. He specialises in the design and production of fine contemporary pieces as well as antique restoration, and is now settled in the USA

PHOTOGRAPHY BY THE AUTHOR
ILLUSTRATIONS BY SIMON RODWAY

The shape of the leg is developed from the traditional cabriole, complementing the curve of the top and rail

This dining table came about largely because I had bought some interesting planks of wild American cherry *(Prunus serotina)* and I wanted to make a piece that would display the unusual grain pattern well. The table, because of its size, would suit a small environment or a kitchen-come-breakfast room.

Construction

The timber was quite warped so I machined short boards for the table top at a usable 20mm (⅞in) or so.

Select your timber for the individual parts and do the basic machining, leaving all the parts at least 100mm (4in) overlength. Face and edge them on the surface planer and then rip to a generous width and thickness, making them 4 to 6mm (¼in) oversize if possible, for later final machining. Put the legs and rails to one side in a dry spot whilst making up the top.

Top

For a finished top thickness of 20mm (⅞in) join the planks that are about 23mm (¹⁵⁄₁₆in) plus thick. Biscuits, dowels and splines can be inserted to help with the alignment. The full width can be glued in one operation if you can work quickly enough, and the result hand-planed to get it flat and thicknessed – which is a lot of work!

An easier method is to join the planks in two stages, gradually building the required width. I have surface and thickness planers that can handle widths up to 450mm (17 ¾in) – so for different capacity machines make suitable adjustments to the following procedure.

The 760mm (30in) wide top is made of six 130mm (5in) wide planks. Edge joint two sets of three boards to make two pieces, about 390mm (15 ⅜in) wide. After glue-up, surface the pieces using light cuts on the surface planer, followed by thicknessing to just a hair over the requisite 20mm (⅞in) – if you scribble over the joined faces with a soft pencil, and when the pencil marks are just gone, you've taken a full cut.

> **"The full width can be glued in one operation if you can work quickly enough, and the result hand-planed to get it flat and thicknessed – which is a lot of work!"**

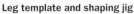
Leg template and shaping jig

ABOVE **Tenons, mortices and leg blanks**

LEFT **Bandsawing legs**

Design

The design work was relatively straightforward being largely determined by the top, in which the twisted grain caused instability, requiring a framework to hold it flat – four rails and legs are ideal.

Some time ago I designed a variation on the cabriole leg consisting of concave curves to the outside faces, and so I used that pattern here. The profile of the leg is complemented by curves in the rail and top – the concavity of the rail provides a visual lift and increases leg room, with the curved edges of the top as a contrast.

The structure being settled, only detailing remained and, with the shape of the leg already to hand, the final design was almost complete. Working within tightly defined strictures is often helpful in speeding the design process because many elements are quickly fixed on.

"To ensure that cutting the mortices, and the shaping, are consistent on each leg, make an I-shaped cradle jig"

Edge joint these two planks so that any step in the thickness is minimal. A little hand-planing and scraping completes the basic job. Sticker the top in a dry place while the rest of the construction is done.

Legs and rails

Turn to the slightly oversize leg and rail materials and get them down to final size on the machines, with the exception of the legs which must be cut to 802mm (31 ½in) – exactly 100mm (4in) longer than their finished length.

This is the time to re-straighten and remove any warping since the parts were first broken out. Normally the next stage is to simply mark and cut the mortices and tenons, but here the process is slightly complicated because of the shaped legs. To ensure that cutting the mortices, and the shaping, are consistent on each leg, make an I-shaped cradle jig, *see sidebar* – this acts as both a pattern and a rod that accurately registers each

leg to transfer essential marks.

Attach the leg blank to the jig and mark the position of the mortice and the leg profile and transfer them to the leg. Remove the leg blank from the jig, cut the mortices, roughly bandsaw the leg to shape, and then re-attach it to the jig. Finally, profile it on the spindle moulder or partially profile it with router and pattern cutting bit.

Mortice and tenon

Place the inside corner of each leg in the jig and screw it in place. Trace round to mark the profile, and transfer the mortice marks to the leg. Repeat for the other three legs. Use square haunched mortices and tenons with the end of the tenon mitred to maximise glue surfaces. You might also use the barefaced tenon, with the bare face to the inside of the leg to increase timber mass.

This is a good time to cut the rails to exact length and mark the curves on the

bottom edge using the two pins and stick method.

Finish marking the legs and rails for the joinery and cut the mortices and tenons. Once this is done, bandsaw the waste from the legs. Cut one face and re-attach the offcuts with masking tape. Cut the second face. Screw each leg back into the jig and use the spindle moulder or a router and pattern cutting bit to follow the profile.

Basic shaping

Complete basic shaping of the legs by marking and cutting the curved inside faces. Make a pattern, offer it up to the inside corner of the legs, trace the shape and cut on the bandsaw. Offcuts from bandsawing the outside curves can be lightly taped in place to balance the leg as it is cut. Clean up machine marks on the legs with a stationary belt sander and hand tools. Round-over the sharp arises with a draw-knife and spokeshaves.

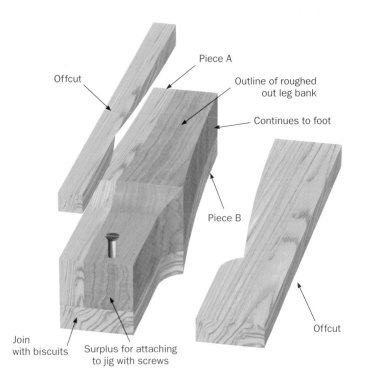

Offcut

Piece A

Outline of roughed
out leg bank

Continues to foot

Piece B

Offcut

Join
with biscuits

Surplus for attaching
to jig with screws

L-shaped cradle jig

To make an L-shaped cradle jig, cut two pieces of 18mm (¾in) ply to 802mm (31½in) long, the same as the leg blank – one of which is 72mm (2⅞in) wide, piece A, and the other 90mm (3½in) wide, piece B.

Dry biscuit the edge of piece A to the face of piece B. Mark a line along the inside of the corner on piece B. Plot the outside profile required on piece A. The profile can be plotted directly, or a full size paper template attached. Cut and smooth the curves – ignoring the inside curve of the leg for now.

Attach this shaped piece to B with countersunk screws. Cut close to the profile with a bandsaw, and trim with a router and pattern cutting bit. Mark the finished length of the leg and the length of the haunched mortice, and square these marks around after assembly.

The tiny rebate on piece A at the inside corner can be formed next, and provides a space for dust. Glue and screw the jig together with biscuits and coutersunk screws. Ensure that the faces are perpendicular to one another. Trim the outside corner flush when dry.

Drill offset countersunk screw holes in each face of the jig into the surplus at the top and bottom of the leg.

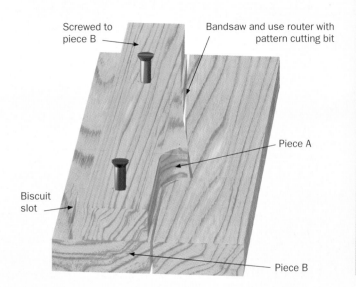

Screwed to
piece B

Bandsaw and use router with
pattern cutting bit

Piece A

Biscuit
slot

Piece B

Buttons and bearers

To hold the top flat to the framework use three buttons at either end. Then make three bearers about 45 by 25mm (1 ¾ by 1in) in section to go across the width to add rigidity. The bearers are made out of three parts. To do similar, cut long pieces with a tongue either end to fit into the channel in the rail. Then rout a channel in the bearer at one end on the underside, about 14mm (½in) square and fit a slip of timber into the channel. Cut the bearer into two parts across the centre of the channel, for attaching to the table top. Bore a suitable clearance hole in the centre of the bearer, and work two extended slots at either end.

Put the bearer in place, fit the slip into the 14mm (½in) square channel and insert four or more screws. Use round-head screws and washers to go through the bearer to attach the top.

I could have simply made the bearers out of one piece of timber, but I chose this three-part method so that the bearers could be fitted after gluing-up the framework rather than during it.

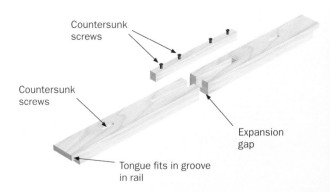

Countersunk
screws

Countersunk
screws

Expansion
gap

Tongue fits in groove
in rail

Cleaning up shape with compass plane

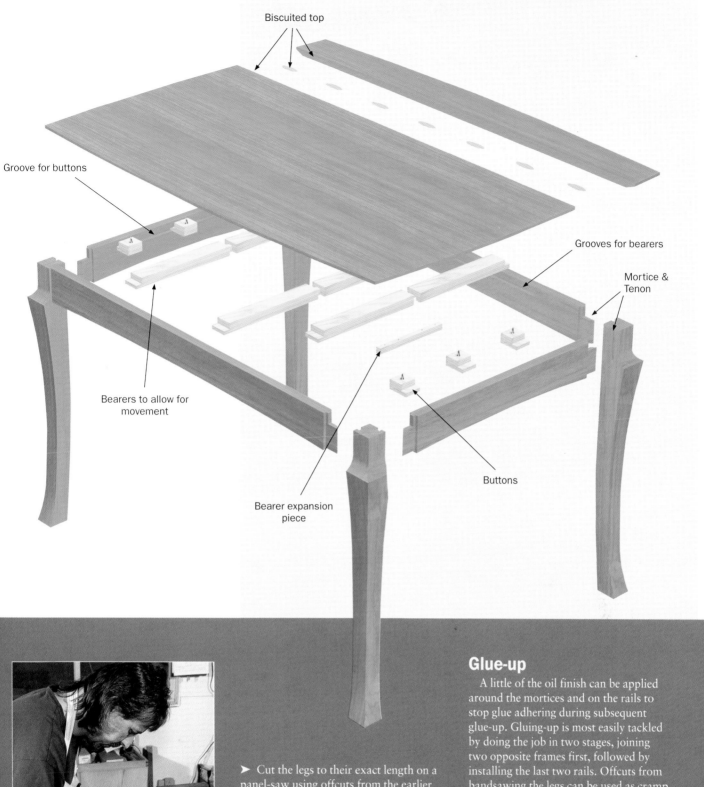

Biscuited top

Groove for buttons

Grooves for bearers

Mortice & Tenon

Bearers to allow for movement

Buttons

Bearer expansion piece

A draw knife is used for chamfer on inside of legs

➤ Cut the legs to their exact length on a panel-saw using offcuts from the earlier bandsawing operations to level them as required.

The curves marked earlier on the bottom edge of the rails can be cut and smoothed with a compass plane or spokeshave. As there are only two of each rail it isn't worth making a pattern to form the curve, but the first rail smoothed can be attached to its opposite partner so as to use a router and pattern cutting bit, and this speeds up the job.

Channels should be routed at this stage to accept buttons and bearers that later hold the top down.

Glue-up

A little of the oil finish can be applied around the mortices and on the rails to stop glue adhering during subsequent glue-up. Gluing-up is most easily tackled by doing the job in two stages, joining two opposite frames first, followed by installing the last two rails. Offcuts from bandsawing the legs can be used as cramp softening blocks.

Planing top

Get the top out, check it is fine to use, and straighten an edge – a no.7 try plane might be easiest if you are working alone or only have a small surface planer – and use this edge to cut it square. Then plot the longest and shortest dimensions both width- and lengthways. Use these plotted dimensions to mark the curves using the two pins and stick method. Cut the curves with a fine bladed jigsaw. Smooth with handplanes.

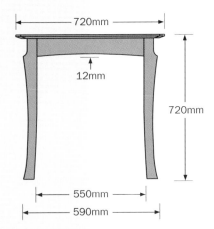

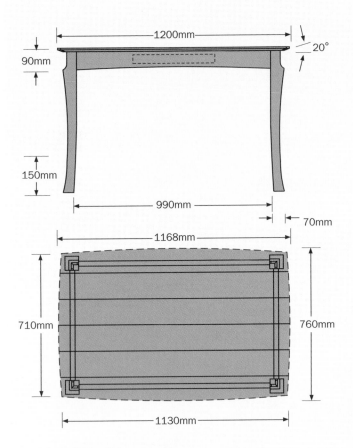

Marking out curve of top

> *"You might also use the barefaced tenon, with the bare face to the inside of the leg to increase timber mass"*

Cutting out top

Turn the top upside down on the bench and mark the bevel on the underside with a pencil gauge, adjustable square, or just mark the line by hand. This bevel can be partially worked with a router, side fence and a variety of cutters, but my favoured method is to tear the material off quickly with a hand-held power planer, doing both the ends first. This way, any tear-out is removed when you cut the long edges. A bit of finishing with hand planes and scrapers completes the job.

Final preparation

Preparing for the application of polish involves hand-planing to remove machine marks, scraping, power sanding, and hand-sanding to both 240 and 320 grit. Only the highly visible table top is sanded to 320 grit – the rest is left at 240. I usually completely prepare all surfaces of the rails and inside faces of the legs prior to glue-up, and final sand the outside faces of the legs later. Because of the twisted and interlocked grain, the table top was sanded on a panel sander from 120 grit to 220 grit, and then completed by hand to 320 grit.

Finish

For the polishing I used 'tung oil finish' which is manufacturers' code for pure tung oil cut with oil varnish and white spirit – US mineral spirit. One strategy is to apply the first coat as it comes out of the can. The second coat is a mix of the tung oil finish, cut with about 10% white spirits, plus 10% oil varnish. Third, and subsequent coats, are a mix of about a third each of tung oil finish, plus white spirits, plus oil varnish.

The technique is to wipe on the finish and buff off with a dry lint-free cloth before it cures too much. Three or four coats applied this way give a smooth satiny, hand-rubbed feel. Light abrasion with 0000 wire wool, or stearated 400 grit paper, in-between coats should be done as needed.

Mike Cowie turned to cabinetmaking after being made redundant five years ago. He took a City & Guilds course at Sheffield College which he passed with distinction, set up his own workshop, and is now in the happy position of having as much work as he can cope with

A hint at Art Deco? Mike finally succumbs to family demands

Recline

PHOTOGRAPHY BY STEPHEN HEPWORTH
ILLUSTRATIONS BY SIMON RODWAY

and fall

Mike Cowie makes a pair of settees for his home

"As from the old saw, the cobbler's children are the last to be shod!" So it's proven with the pair of settees featured here. This project's been under way for approximately two years – more off than on – and because they're for our own use, pressure of work has unfortunately cast them to one side on more than one occasion. My dear wife, stoic as ever, my daughter less so, preferring orange boxes to the indignity of bringing friends home, given the old suite these settees would replace.

Having arrived at the conclusion we

were in need of a replacement suite, viewing new ones was a salutary lesson. Those we saw were of poor quality with garish colours, and anything half-way decent was out of reach financially. Therefore, someone had the bright idea of making one!

Concept and preparation

Bearing in mind the least durable part is the material – hence there's so many reupholstery firms – how about making a solid wood frame with loose

cushions that can be replaced as necessary? That's easy then, with instructions received work can commence. Well almost!

With no client to please it should be a simple matter to design something suitable. However, this had been handed over by the family to me, a practised procrastinator. Eventually, a satisfactory doodle established a starting point, this being essentially an outline of a flared back model with solid rounded legs. Any details only help to confuse, so I trusted my

Front on, showing arm detail

intuition for the remainder of the piece.

American ash (*Fraxinus americana*) was the chosen wood: light, clean looking and reasonably priced. The arms were to be almost 100mm (4in) thick yet the thought of carrying and working 100mm (4in) timber provided sufficient incentive to purchase 50mm (2in) material and glue up to the desired thickness. One of my more enlightened decisions which worked wonderfully well – almost!

Having planed up the timber and using a template to mark out the outline cut out on the bandsaw. Eight pieces with four fronts are carefully selected for grain match. It was only afterwards I discovered I'd glued up for four right hand arms, hence the discrepancy with the grain left to right.

I've recently been watching Tate Modern on television, initially out of a sense of duty to try and understand modern art, the artist and what motivates the purchaser. I failed. However, I realised if I continued to make these

damn silly mistakes I'll eventually have the opportunity of displaying one of my pieces.

Construction

The arms, having been glued up, now require trimming back. This is where a steady hand on the bandsaw pays dividends. The template is pinned to the arm and a guide bush fitted to the router, a Ryobi 3hp with plenty of power. Progressive cuts are then made providing a smooth finish. Mortices are cut with a 19mm (³/4in) chisel, first constructing a simple jig to hold the arms at the same angle. Now I can begin work on the front rail, cut from 50mm (2in) ash. As on the smaller settee the grain perfectly suited this piece: compressed in the centre, flowing out at either end. The arc is determined by the well proven method of a thin slat bent between two points, scribed along and cut out on the bandsaw; the ripples removed with a spokeshave and finished with a belt sander.

I now favour cutting out tenons roughly to size on the bandsaw, finishing off with the router. Leaving the front at this stage and moving on to the back legs, as there might be insufficient American ash, I selected some English ash (*Fraxinus excelsior*) for straight grain and then laminate to thickness.

The legs are tapered from top to bottom, starting at 50mm (2in) reducing to 38mm (1¹/2in) at the top. As for the front legs, I make a template so each remain equal and then cut out on the bandsaw; cleaning up afterwards with plane, spokeshave and belt sander. I know there are people who view this tool with horror. However, used with care I find it to be a real boon.

Trim and cut

As with the front rail, the legs are morticed using a jig to keep the correct angle. Now to cutting out the back rail on the bandsaw, the inside curve first with a marking gauge to mark the

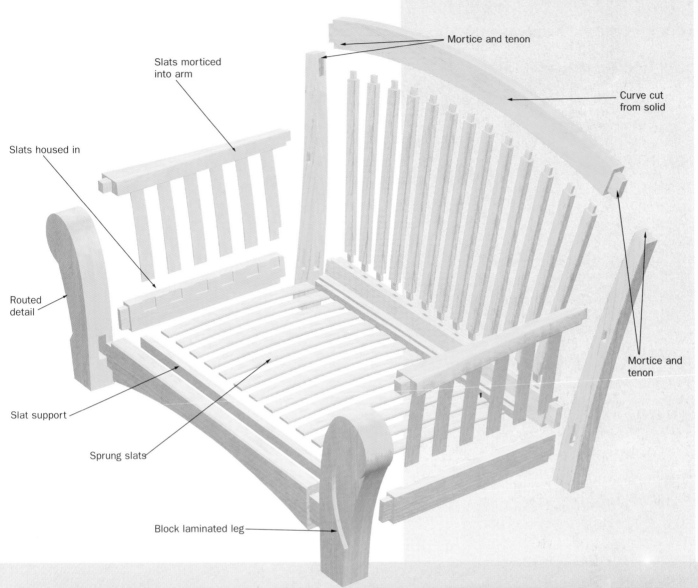

Mortice and tenon

Slats morticed into arm

Curve cut from solid

Slats housed in

Routed detail

Slat support

Sprung slats

Mortice and tenon

Block laminated leg

Side detail

Back slats and rail

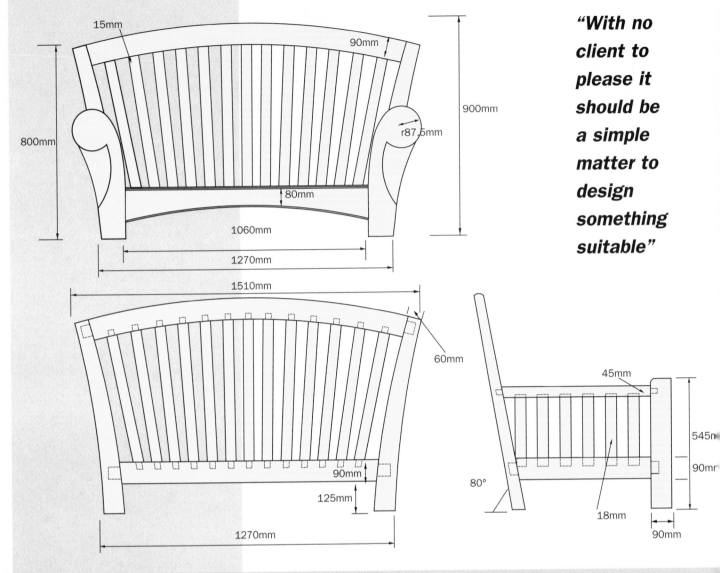

cutting line of the outside curve. After cleaning up, the back legs are laid on the floor at the right angle; the top and bottom rail placed on top with the shoulders marked directly allowing the rails to be tenoned.

Trimming the tenons to size a dry fit is achieved, then stood up with the front legs and checked for appearance – this looked about right. The back supports are mostly cut out from the waste resulting from the curved rails, planed to 22mm (7/8in) thick.

For the fitting, a centre line is scribed on the top and bottom rail. Using this as the first line, a rail is placed across, the position of the shoulders marked on the vertical support rail while the position of this rail is marked upon the top and bottom rail for morticing. Each rail is spaced and marked individually with each one numbered. Mortices are cut with the router; the tenons cut and a dry fit attempted – this can be fun with so many different lengths. Make any

alterations until a close fit is achieved. Tedious, I know, but necessary!

Chamfers

A small chamfer was taken off the rails ending with a full radius. Chamfers are then taken off the top and bottom rails – with the router – whilst the back legs are reduced to the desired taper. Then bandsaw as usual to finish with chamfers off all edges to neaten up and give a uniform look all round. A passover with the orbital sander left the back ready for glue up and, with experience being a good tutor, this is done in stages: the top, bottom and support rails first; with a check on the diagonals for square – or should that be symmetrical? When these had set, the legs are added, making a relatively trouble free glue up, which is a nice change!

Assembly

Arriving at this stage was as far as my thinking had gone. I now had to

consider how to link the front with the back. Various combinations are tried: rounded, flowing arms, both low and high. However, often the simple answer can prove the best, certainly the most expedient. In this case, a straight arm with a curve cut on the outside. The lower side rail was quite simple, just an educated guess as to the depth, front to back and the amount of angle necessary. Having decided this, a sliding bevel is used to mark the shoulders with tenons cut out first due to the curves on the front and back legs. Using a square set to the bottom of the legs, a perpendicular line is scribed up the legs, setting a parallel line with the marking gauge. To intersect this, a base is formed with which to plant the tenon on, then scribe round and mortice with a mallet and chisel, having first removed the majority of waste with a Forstner bit. Hand made indeed! There's still a bit of travel in this debate as to what constitutes hand

Whole back view

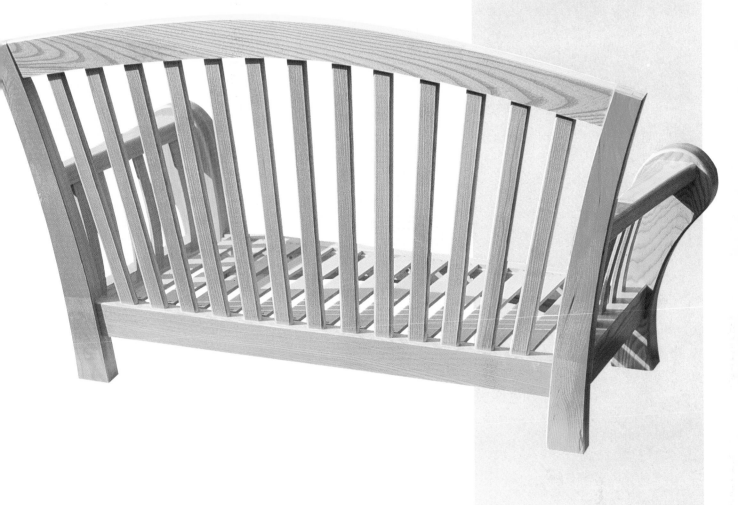

made. And I often find myself imagining looking over the shoulder of an 18th century craftsman at work at the bench to observe the methods employed in the practice of his craft.

Back to work

The bottom side rails are fitted in place and a measure taken of the distance between, front to back, at the desired height of the arm rest. Allowing 38mm (1½in) for the front tenon and 32mm (1¼in) for the rear tenon, the arm rests are cut to length and the tenons cut using the bevel for the rear shoulders; for morticing the bottom rail the same method is used. A trial fit ensured all are correct.

Side slips are required to keep the cushions in place and for these I planed some ash strips to 6mm (¼in) thick, cutting mortices to suit on the underside of the armrest with the router and matched stopped grooves cut on the bottom rail to accommodate.

I pinned my faith in the strength of the tenons on the arm rest, my intention being to inset the slips into the mortices and cramp the bottom firmly in place in the stopped groove creating a slightly rounded profile to match the front leg. These, however, are one of the last pieces to be fitted hence it's wait and see.

Front legs

Back to the front legs for a final touch before glueing up. My intention had been to carve a volute scroll on the front face. With time in short supply an alternative method of decoration is adopted. Namely, creating a shadow line by the removal of a section, highlighting the round face and, hopefully, making an otherwise bulky leg appear less so. Using the template made for cutting out the legs, first carrying the line around the curve and then using the side of the template, draw a line arcing down the side. Using these guide

lines, a bush is fitted to the router, the template clamped to the work and progressive cuts are made to a depth of 12mm (½in) around the lines. Then, using the Ryobi fitted with a 12mm (½in) bottom cut bit and working from the outside edge in, the waste is nibbled away. Working inwards ensures there's always a firm base with which to work on. This completed, a scraper is used to smooth the surface.

Front rail and finishing

The front rail received a stopped chamfer along the underside, the full one on top with the arm rest, whilst having started out square, is rounded off on the inside face, the outer receiving a curve, giving a more pleasing appearance.

With the majority of the work now complete a finish is applied prior to glueing up. I chose a water based lacquer mainly for its non-yellowing properties. Unfortunately, Danish oil applied to ash robs it of its nice clean

Mike's favourite router

Routing

If I might add a brief word regarding routers...

Whilst learning the craft I was greatly impressed watching Ramon Weston demonstrating the Leigh jig, though it wasn't the jig that received all the attention, rather the router used – the Festo OF900. The main characteristic of this tool is the single hand pistol grip, the only router I'd seen at the time with this style of grip. I was intrigued by this. My router purchase to date had been the big 3hp Ryobi, a router almost – though not quite! – impossible to use single handedly.

Having purchased the Festo, complete with dust extractor, this has been the mainstay of my work for three years now. I mention this because I frequently hear about people who, having purchased a router, refrain from using it through apprehension, even fear. The Festo, although costly, is a safe user-friendly router and so versatile I feel it deserves a wider audience.

"The addition of slightly sprung slats on the base – cut slightly large to give a convex aspect – completed the construction of the smaller settee"

Back frame ready for fitting into leg mortices

Close up of routed leg detail

looks. Water based lacquer has its disadvantages though; it raises the grain – being water based it would, wouldn't it! Also, being so quick drying, brush strokes show unless a good quality lacquer brush is used – there's something to be said for spraying here.

I use a lacquer brush and apply three coats; rubbing down between each coat a pleasant finish is obtained. The reason for applying a finish before gluing up is so the rubbing down between each coat is more efficient, avoiding unsightly build up of lacquer in the corners.

Assembly

Now the frame can be assembled, scraping off the lacquer around the mortices for good adhesion, glued and clamped together. The only difficulty now being trying to manoeuvre it through the house, having glued it up outside on a sunny Saturday afternoon

– a point not to be neglected!

A big, solid, heavy settee carcass is now awaiting the side slips. These are cut to length, inserted into the mortices one at a time, glued in place and left to set with a nice curve to match the front arm the result.

The addition of slightly sprung slats on the base – cut slightly large to give a convex aspect – completed the construction of the smaller settee. The large one differed only in the curves of the front and back rails; a rather flatter curve resulting due to the extra length.

Upholstery?

All that remains to complete the pair of settees is the upholstery. This is the point where *we* – the family – come back into the equation as my choice is obviously not to be trusted. At the time of writing – having a well deserved break in Ullswater with no phones or workshop – we're still looking!

PHOTOGRAPHY BY ROBERT SEYMOUR
ILLUSTRATIONS BY SIMON RODWAY

The table has a contemporary feel whilst using traditional techniques

Robert Chapman is a chartered civil engineer who retired from a career in local government in 1997. Since then he has developed a long-standing interest in woodworking

Trad goes modern

Robert Chapman makes a coffee table with drawers

W hen I am making a piece I find the design process as much of a challenge as the subsequent construction. Furniture-making principles have evolved over thousands of years and a range of structural disciplines exist which have to be maintained – and any originality has to respect these rules. However, having come to this activity rather late in life, and not yet having worked commercially, I see myself following a self-imposed apprenticeship in which mistakes have to be made and then rectified – hopefully with pleasing results.

Timber preparation

All major components are cut and planed oversize and allowed to settle for

"With so many components for such a small piece, the order of batting for glue-up is critical"

as long as possible. The drawer linings and table top are among the items first dealt with. In practice, everything remained remarkably stable and a little corrective work was necessary, but the drawer linings were re-sawn from a 20mm (¾in) board and I needed to give them as much time as possible to stabilise.

Legs and aprons

I decided to use haunched double tenons for the side and rear aprons. The mortices for these were drilled out and then completed by hand, having

previously prepared the legs to precise dimensions. The tenons were initially cut on the bandsaw and finished by hand.

Drawer rails

The top drawer rail is half-lap dovetailed into the top of the front legs while the bottom rail is held with a pair of stub tenons to maximise the glue surface area. The drawer spacers are located between the upper and lower rails by wedged tenons, and a tongue is created on the rear face of the spacers to position the drawer dividers which

Prototypes

So far, each piece, and this table is no exception, has been a prototype and, to a limited extent, the design has to evolve with the construction. Also, I have limited space and machinery which place constraints on the work I undertake.

If I were to operate commercially, things would have to change or I would very soon go out of business but I enjoy working as I do, particularly when things go well, even if it is in a sense unashamedly self-indulgent.

The coffee table with drawers was a family request – the drawers were needed to provide storage for a growing range of remote control devices and associated paraphernalia.

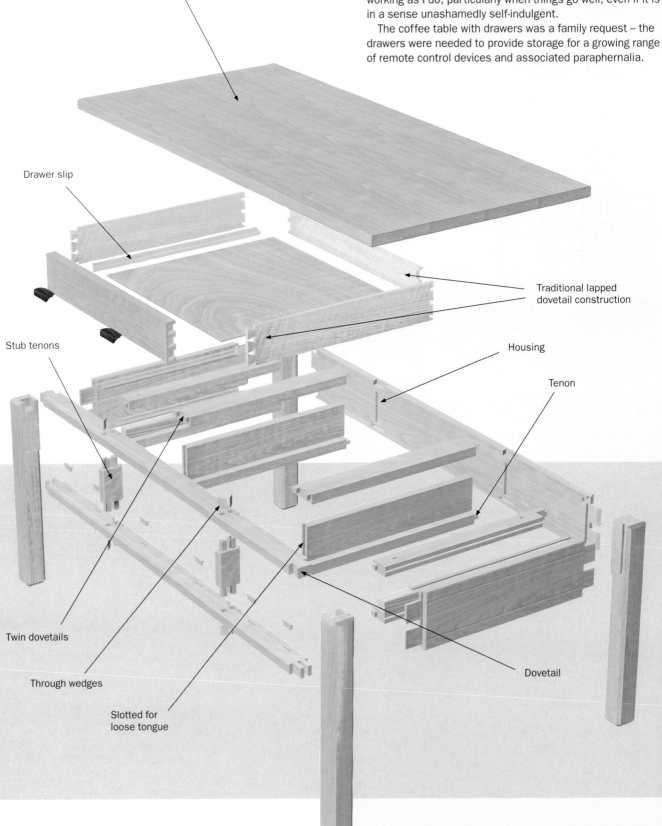

Top butt jointed

Drawer slip

Traditional lapped dovetail construction

Stub tenons

Housing

Tenon

Twin dovetails

Through wedges

Slotted for loose tongue

Dovetail

Timber

The American black walnut *(Juglans nigra)* looks stylish and is appropriate for its proposed surroundings – it was also readily available and reasonably easy to work. Quarter-sawn oak *(Quercus spp)* was used for the drawer linings while cedar of Lebanon *(Cedrus libani)* was selected for the drawer bottoms. The drawer pulls were made from ebony *(Diospryros spp)*. I wanted the construction of the table to follow broadly traditional lines for both the main structure and the drawers.

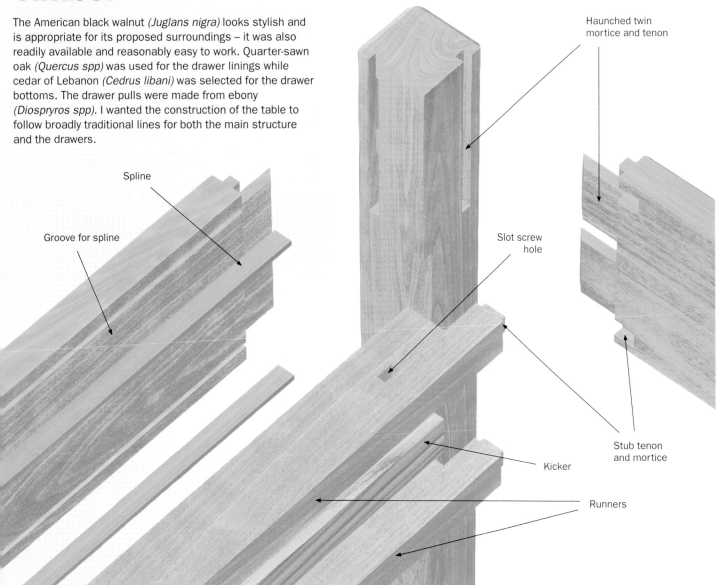

Spline

Groove for spline

Haunched twin mortice and tenon

Slot screw hole

Stub tenon and mortice

Kicker

Runners

---

are also located in housings in the rear apron. These are assembled and fixed later – mortices for the spacers are cut at this stage.

Preparation

Finally, before commencing glue-up, a number of small but essential operations have to be completed – these include the mortices for the stub tenons supporting the outer drawer runners and kickers, any similar work for drawer stops and buttons, the groove for the ply splines in the side aprons, and the housings for the divider units in the rear apron.

In all these instances the depth of cut is relatively shallow and the work can be undertaken either on the router table or with the router in conventional mode.

All chamfers must also be cut to the legs, aprons and rails, taking care to stop the chamfer on the inside corner of the legs, short of the apron. Again the router is the most suitable tool for this activity. All these small tasks are so easily forgotten and I find it pays to painstakingly list them before contemplating a glue-up. Putting things right later is, at best, a nuisance.

Sub-frame assembly

With so many components for such a small piece, the order of batting for glue-up is critical. In this case, the front and back components were assembled first, followed by the ends, and finally, the divider units complete with runners and kickers.

The glue-up for me is always a bit of a nightmare and needs to be practised to ensure everything is at hand. I also keep the number of components being glued to a minimum to reduce the chances of catastrophe.

Front frame

Indeed, while the back frame is straightforward, the front frame is not, and another pair of hands would be helpful, particularly when tapping in the wedges. The outer runners and kickers are glued to the side aprons before joining to the completed front and rear assemblies remembering first to cut the countersunk slots in the kickers to hold the table top. The divider units with runners and kickers are then assembled

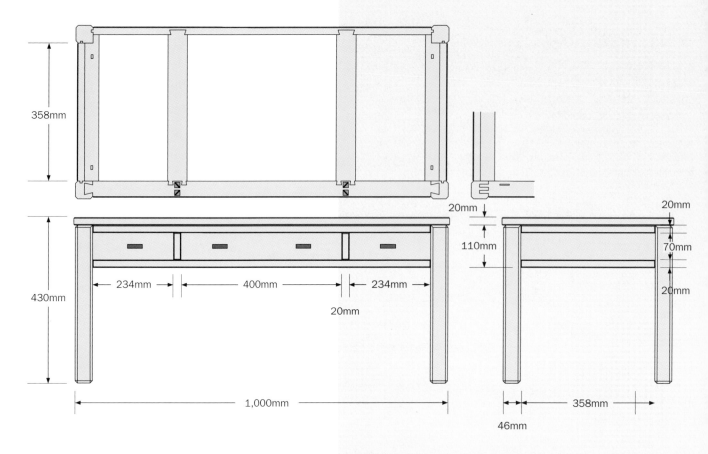

358mm

20mm

20mm

110mm

70mm

430mm

234mm — 400mm — 234mm

20mm

20mm

1,000mm

358mm

46mm

"Indeed, while the back frame is straightforward, the front frame is not, and another pair of hands would be helpful"

in situ within the rigid completed framework. It is worth noting that the dividers also act as drawer guides and these can be given the smallest of tapers, from front to back to aid later drawer fitting. This applies equally to the guides at each end of the table which are glued and screwed to the aprons. Whatever happens, the space between the guides must not be narrower at the back than the front or a satisfactory drawer fit will be impossible.

Drawers

The drawers are entirely traditional – the linings are quarter-sawn oak, 8.5mm (¹¹⁄₃₂in) thick, lap-dovetailed at the front and through-dovetailed at the back. Drawer slips, also in oak, then ➤

The chamfer detail is designed to catch the light and create interest

Drawer pulls

It may seem a very small point but the drawer pulls were the subject of much thought. Proprietary products would, for the most part, have looked out of place. Turned knobs could have worked but I preferred something that reflected the overall proportions of the piece. Hence the finished product was made from ebony in a long length, the profile being formed with both the router and moulding planes. The individual drawer pulls were cut to length, chamfered and burnished prior to fitting with a tongue at the back which fits into the mortices in the drawer fronts. The pulls are equally spaced along the front and the dimensions reflect the overall proportions of the table.

Drawer construction is traditional, complete with slips and quarter-sawn oak sides

"Drawer fitting follows the usual patient approach, adjusting a little at a time until a smooth fit is achieved"

Self-indulgence

It had been my original intention to have the table top set back on the frame by the chamfer width on the top of the legs, but when I tried the alternative with a slightly larger top I felt it was preferable – the chamfers still catch the light and create interest.

Perhaps one day I will make an alternative top to the original dimensions with a burr veneer framed in black walnut – now that really would be self-indulgent.

➤ hold the bottom where cedar of Lebanon is used. Rebates in the front and sides of the drawer bottoms engage with grooves in the slips and the drawer front. They are held by glue only at the front and by slot screws into the back of the drawer to allow for movement. Drawer fitting follows the usual patient approach, adjusting a little at a time until a smooth fit is achieved, and at this point I also fitted the drawer stops to the mortices in the lower rail.

"The edge profile is completed with a tiny rebate on the underside to disguise any future movement"

Top

I had left the final preparation of the top until this stage. The boards I had chosen and roughly prepared earlier had moved only a small amount so corrective work was limited. The four boards making up the top are matched for grain as far as possible, planed fractionally hollow, and firstly glued up in pairs, finishing a little oversize, before trimming and chamfering. The edge profile is completed with a tiny rebate on the underside to disguise any future movement. It is then fixed with slot screws and buttons in the traditional way. Access to screws in a shallow table top can be a problem but can be overcome with the aid of a small cranked ratchet screwdriver.

Finishing

The inside surfaces of the drawers, but not the bottoms, are finished with shellac prior to glue-up to ease the removal of any excess glue. All exposed surfaces of the table are given several coats of finishing oil diluted 50:50 with white spirit. Any surplus oil must be wiped away fairly soon after application. The table top requires more applications to achieve a good result and it is then given a light coat of wax.

PHOTOGRAPHY BY STEPHEN HEPWORTH
ILLUSTRATIONS BY IAN HALL (MAIN)
AND SIMON RODWAY

Mike Cowie turned to cabinetmaking
after being made redundant five years
ago. He took a City & Guilds course at
Sheffield College which he passed
with distinction; set up his own
workshop, and is now in the happy
position of having as much work as he
can cope with

Mike Cowie

makes a walnut
semicircular table

**Some inspiring figure
and speculation
produced this table**

A piece
of luck

An English semicircular table for
one penny! Well not quite,
though the penny certainly was
the motivating factor...

Included with an electric bill from our
local supplier was an offer to purchase
the Yorkshire Post for 1p. My wife and I
both liked the look of the paper so
decided to accept the offer. In the Post,
as though by fate, was an advertisement
for a walnut *(Juglans sp)* tree for sale.
Procrastination set in - the thought of
spending all that money - though after

eventually telephoning on the Saturday
evening I discovered the wood was,
fortunately, still available. After
arranging to call on the Sunday
morning, I learned the story behind the
tree – a tale I still view with incredulity,
particularly in this day and age – as here
was a tree approaching 300 years old!

The tree had been felled in Hessle
cemetery for reasons unknown – safety
probably. However, there it lay awaiting
the chainsaw and bonfire. Fortunately, it
was spotted, haggled over, bought and

cut into usable sections by an old sawyer
ready for retirement. Thereafter it was
laid down for air drying where it
remained for ten years. A decision to
return to teaching prompted the owner
to place the advert; thus I became the
owner of a 300 year old walnut tree –
the likes of which must be extremely rare
in Britain today – saved from the
bonfire!

The semicircular table – or demi lune
to clients, it sounds better – remains to
date one of only three things made with
the walnut. In truth, I had been itching
to make something with it and this style
of table seemed appropriate.

Construction

To begin, the legs were rough cut from
40mm (1⅝in) stock and left inside to
acclimatise. This subsequently appears
unnecessary as the long period of air

The walnut in question

"Thus I became the owner of a 300 year old walnut tree – the likes of which must be extremely rare in Britain today – saved from the bonfire"

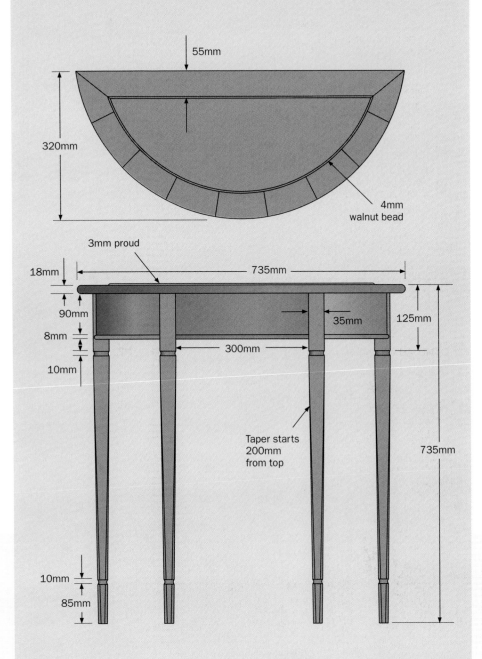

55mm

320mm

4mm
walnut bead

3mm proud

18mm

735mm

90mm

35mm

125mm

8mm

300mm

10mm

Taper starts
200mm
from top

735mm

10mm

85mm

drying seems to have eliminated all stresses – however, best to be safe. Whilst waiting for the legs, the skirt can be constructed – *see panel*. The method I chose was to laminate around a plywood former; the plywood bought at a local auction, some 200 pieces of 635 by 460 by 19mm (25 by 18 by ¾in) for 10 pence each! This is ideal for making formers and the like. The shape is determined by scribing an arc then shortening the ends making it more elliptical – this I consider necessary due to the shallow depth of the table.

Edging

The back is butt-jointed into rebates; cut on the ends of the skirt, glued up and strengthened with fillets glued on the inside – a central spar was added for strength. The skirt is used to form a template for the top, laying it on a piece of ply and using a 35mm (1⅜in) block, drawing around this and cutting out. Working from the template the edging, which is solid walnut, is formed into

segments allowing the grain to flow round. Each segment is then grooved with a bearing mounted cutter on the router, keeping well back from the edge. The edging is then glued up with plywood splines inserted into the grooves – this to aid strength for it is end grain to be glued. Rubbed joints proved adequate. The back is left loose at this stage, the outer edge trimmed to shape via the ply template and a bearing mounted cutter in the router. A template can be made to form the inside curve; however, for speed, I chose to trim to size using the fence not the easiest method for curves.

Table top

With this operation complete, the ends can be mitred to the back also grooving around the inside for the table top. The top is a piece of ply or MDF veneered with walnut: thin strips cut on the bandsaw and jointed together then veneered using my special press – two pieces of 50mm (2in) work top with plenty of cramps. It works well though I'm saving for a vacuum press! The top is shaped to fit allowing a lip to fit into the grooves created with the router; the whole than glued together, planed and sanded flush round off the edge. Finally, rout out a 4mm (⁵⁄₃₂in) groove to accommodate the beading. This ➤

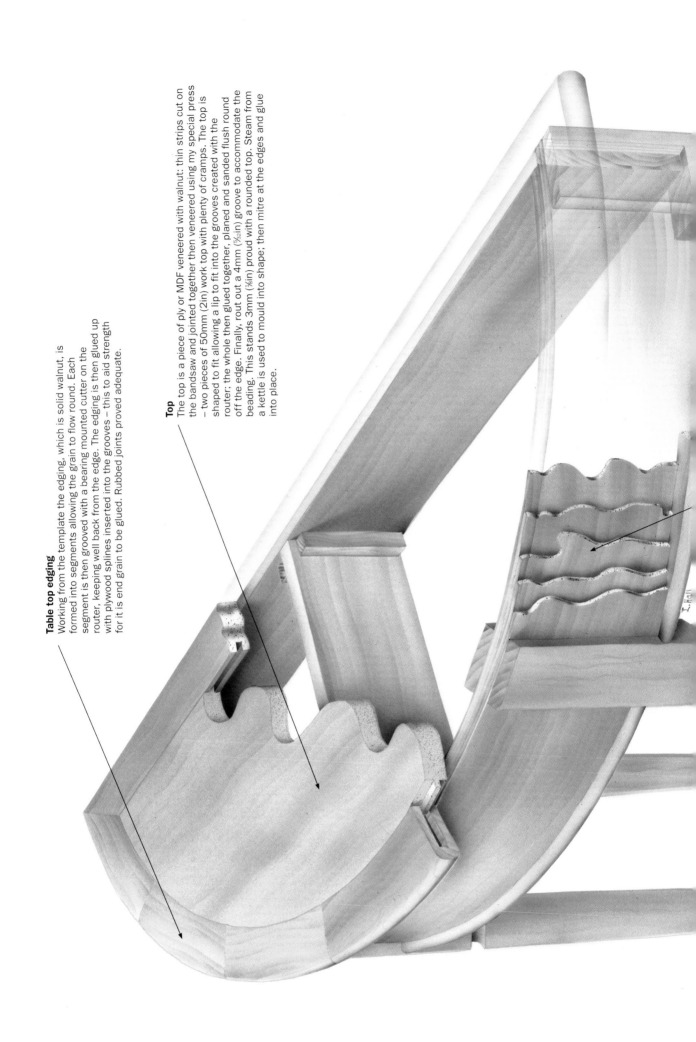

Table top edging
Working from the template the edging, which is solid walnut, is formed into segments allowing the grain to flow round. Each segment is then grooved with a bearing mounted cutter on the router, keeping well back from the edge. The edging is then glued up with plywood splines inserted into the grooves – this to aid strength for it is end grain to be glued. Rubbed joints proved adequate.

Top
The top is a piece of ply or MDF veneered with walnut: thin strips cut on the bandsaw and jointed together then veneered using my special press – two pieces of 50mm (2in) work top with plenty of cramps. The top is shaped to fit allowing a lip to fit into the grooves created with the router; the whole then glued together, planed and sanded flush round off the edge. Finally, rout out a 4mm (⁵⁄₃₂in) groove to accommodate the beading. This stands 3mm (⅛in) proud with a rounded top. Steam from a kettle is used to mould into shape; then mitre at the edges and glue into place.

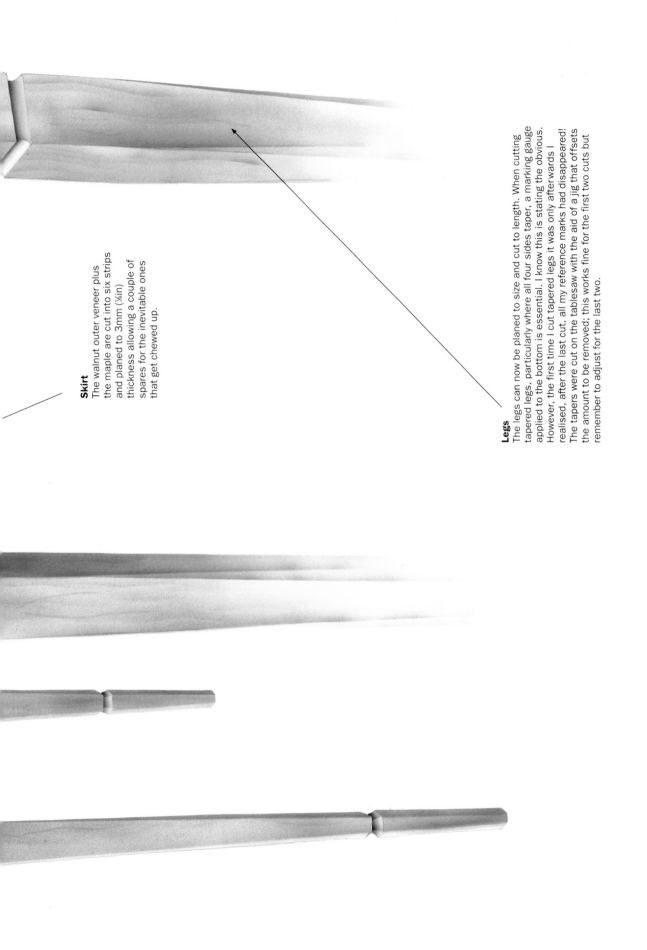

Skirt
The walnut outer veneer plus the maple are cut into six strips and planed to 3mm (⅛in) thickness allowing a couple of spares for the inevitable ones that get chewed up.

Legs
The legs can now be planed to size and cut to length. When cutting tapered legs, particularly where all four sides taper, a marking gauge applied to the bottom is essential. I know this is stating the obvious. However, the first time I cut tapered legs it was only afterwards I realised, after the last cut, all my reference marks had disappeared! The tapers were cut on the tablesaw with the aid of a jig that offsets the amount to be removed; this works fine for the first two cuts but remember to adjust for the last two.

Laminating

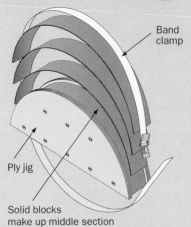

Band clamp

Ply jig

Solid blocks make up middle section

Two pieces of ply are cut to the required shape and joined together with bridging pieces giving a platform 95mm (3¾in) wide upon which to form the skirt. Side guides, I find, are essential for such work in order that the laminations stay where intended. Unwilling to cut up more walnut than necessary a secondary wood is used for the majority of the work; in this case some field maple *(Acer sp)* that I happened to have on hand – at least I think it was!

The walnut outer veneer plus the maple are cut into strips and planed to 3mm (⅛in) thickness allowing a couple of spares for the inevitable ones that get chewed up. Five strips of maple with the top veneer of walnut; a pot of Cascamite mixed to a nice creamy consistency; glue brush ready and not forgetting to fasten the former securely to either trestles or the bench – I've tried without and, believe me, it's rather sad. All that effort! However, if you enjoy a challenge be my guest. The clamp was one of those broad material types – lorry fasteners, with a ratchet for fastening, the slack first being taken up by a mixture of hands, knees and bad grace – until eventually reaching the point where the spanner can be brought into play.

As a precaution, a strip of maple is placed between the walnut and strap to avoid any pressure ridges forming, also plenty of wax is applied to aid removal. This is left overnight to set, removed and planed to size, and cut to length

Details of the Jorgensen 6200 band clamp used in this Project can be obtained from Chesterman Marketing on: 01785 250341.

Speculation worked – the table sold!

➤ stands 3mm (⅛in) proud with a rounded top. Steam from a kettle is used to mould into shape; then mitre at the edges and glue into place.

Making the legs

The legs can now be planed to size and cut to length with the first task to rout out a hollow with a 10mm (⅜in) cove cutter. Lining up all the legs together made this an easy task using the fence, turning in sequence until complete. When cutting tapered legs, particularly where all four sides taper, a marking gauge applied to the bottom is essential. I know this is stating the obvious. However, the first time I cut tapered legs it was only afterwards I realised, after the last cut, all my reference marks had disappeared!

The tapers were cut on the tablesaw with the aid of a jig that offsets the amount to be removed, works fine for the first two cuts but remember to adjust for the last two. Clean up to the scribed marks at the bottom. The cove cuts on the bottom, unfortunately, have to be cut individually – a shame, but a small jig that holds the leg in place allowing the

router fence to be used proves easily constructed. The square leg has now to be converted to octagonal starting from just below the upper coves, a jack plane proved the easiest solution gauging the cuts by eye, with a round file completing the coves.

Completion

I attached the legs to the skirt via a bridle joint, cut on the two centre legs, with lap joints on the two outer legs and glued in place, with a screw for the two outer legs – just in case! All this with great difficulty, mind.

The beading is then cut to size and fitted on the bottom of the skirt. Gluing this in place completes the construction. Finally, a good clean up and French polish – not my favourite finish, though this speaks more for my technique than the polish – however, the walnut responded extremely well.

The table, while a speculative piece, was well received at a display in Doncaster and purchased by Mr and Mrs Lindley, an architect and his wife, bringing in further interest and orders for similar pieces.

The light coloured but interesting figure of the ash gives a modern feel to the traditional detail of this dining suite

Mark Constanduros has been making furniture since the age of 10 and received his first commission at the age of 15. He completed a two year design/making course at Rycotewood College, Oxfordshire, followed by a one year BADA Furniture Restoration course at West Dean, Chichester. Mark started his own business in 1994 and shares a workshop with two other makers

PHOTOGRAPHY BY ANTHONY BAILEY

Mark Constanduros makes a dining room suite – part one

The full monty

The brief

It's not everyday the opportunity to make an entire set of furniture for a single room comes along – if you're lucky you might get to make some pieces to be scattered around a client's house. This was my chance to make a dining table 2440 by 1525mm (8 by 5ft) with ten dining chairs; a serving table; sideboard and a small lamp table to finish the set! The design requirements made by the client were fairly clear: not too traditional and not too modern, just clean, fresh and simple.

The client's dining room is fairly large and could accept a table of this size. My first idea was a refectory style table, due to the fact the room could accommodate a large table, but I didn't want it to look like a great solid cube of wood sitting in the room. The refectory style table is traditional but, to modernise it, my suggestion of making it in ash *(Fraxinus*

sp), which is not too plain, with walnut *(Juglans sp)* for the detailing, was enthusiastically received.

The other great idea was that due to the client's large family we thought the serving table could be used as an extension to the dining table, taking it to 3050 by 1525mm (10 by 5ft). This gave the serving table dual use rather than just sitting in the corner looking pretty.

The dining table

My first thought concerned the dining table's size – a solid top 2440 by 1525mm (8 by 5ft) – is a large expanse to cover. I find that it really does pay to spend time at your local sawmill sorting through the boards, especially in this case where the timber will be the star. I nearly always try to buy consecutive boards and sometimes an entire tree to ensure the same colour throughout; though with ash you get the olive

towards the centre boards which in larger trees can dominate the board. The smaller the tree, the less of chance of olive creeping in.

I had decided on the width of the boards for the top before reaching the sawmill. I felt that seven boards would be possible for the dining table and, as it happened, I was able to bookmatch the boards using a busy grained board as the middle and pairing the others up from consecutive boards. For the serving table two boards was sufficient, as the grain was really busy.

"It's not everyday the opportunity to make an entire set of furniture for a single room comes along"

Refectory style

The side table doubles as an extension to this already huge table

Small walnut details like this plug add subtle decoration

Top construction, plywood tongue and plug

Decorative detail: plugs, chamfers and beading

The table legs were a problem, having to come from 150mm (6in) timber and not many sawmills had wood kiln dried at this thickness. This was overcome by a trip to Wiltshire – though, usually, you'll probably have to buy twice as much to ensure you get a piece with as few faults as possible.

Construction

On to the making...With the boards chosen for the tops I rough machined them first so I knew there was as little olive on the top surface as possible, and that I could safely use the other boards for the frame. With the tops sandwiched together and covered, so the moisture

could not reach them, I then set about making the frame.

Due to the serving table and dining table being the same height and design, I machined the legs together so I could pick the better legs at 90 by 90mm (3½ by 3½in) for the dining table. Those that had traces of olive could be machined down to 65 by 65mm (2⅝ by 2⅝in) for the serving table. Again, all the legs were cut to length at the same time and all the mortices cut together; though the ones on the dining table were slightly wider – but using the same mortice bit.

The Wadkin DM morticer that I use has an attachment for up to nine different stop settings. I only marked

one leg and cramped a stop to the morticer fence so that all the legs were in the same place. This proved a valuable addition to the machine once you gained its trust, as there are no pencil lines to follow.

With all the mortices chiselled out, machine up the rails and mark out the tenons. I cut these on a tenoner – then you can cut the shoulders back.

All the top rails of the tables had a 10mm (⅜in) beaded edge moulding running along the bottom edge. These were cut on the spindle moulder, making sure that the top of the bead was below the surface of the rail; otherwise when it comes to sanding you'll flatten off the top of the bead.

The stretcher rails all had a 9mm (1½in) bull nose on the edges, as common with tables. Inevitably, people's feet knock the edge which becomes ragged over time.

> "Traditionally, all the joints were dowel pegged, but for this particular piece the square walnut pegs are there for decoration"

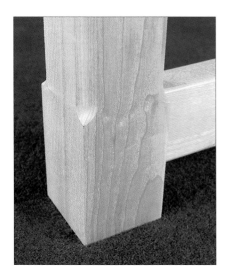

Leg chamfer meeting stretcher rail

Buttons

To fix the tops to the main frame, the easiest and nicest way is to use 'buttons'. The button will allow the table to expand and contract, as well as keep the top securely in place. Just remember not to put the button tight into the groove thus restricting movement.

Buttons vary in size depending on the item of furniture but for the dining table a size rather larger than average was required and a number 12 size screw. Normally, I would use brass screws but they tend to be too soft these days and I have reverted to use bronze Posi-drives. Due to the power in the timber on this particular

'Buttons' hold down the top

table they gave the required amount of grip needed to hold the top down to the frame.

I used the same size button on the serving table purely because it was easier to make extra of one size.

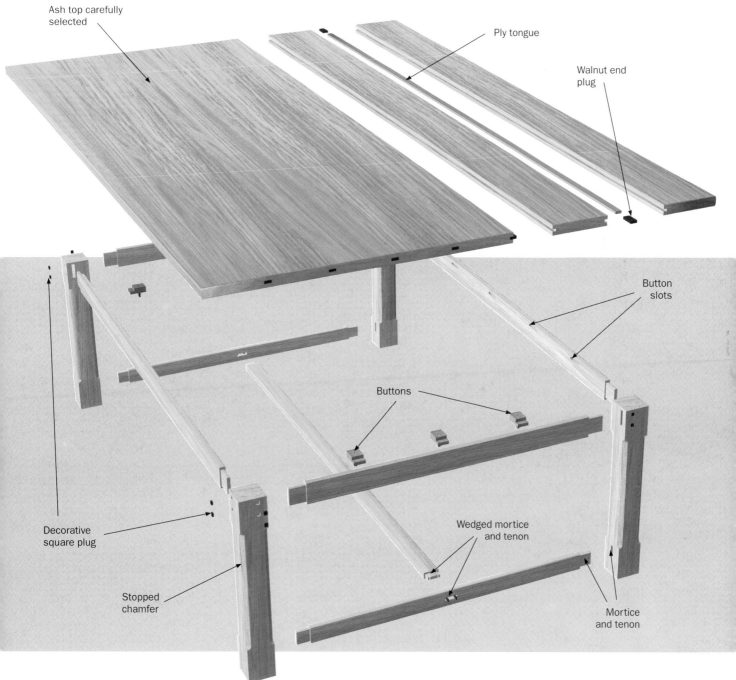

Ash top carefully selected

Ply tongue

Walnut end plug

Button slots

Buttons

Decorative square plug

Stopped chamfer

Wedged mortice and tenon

Mortice and tenon

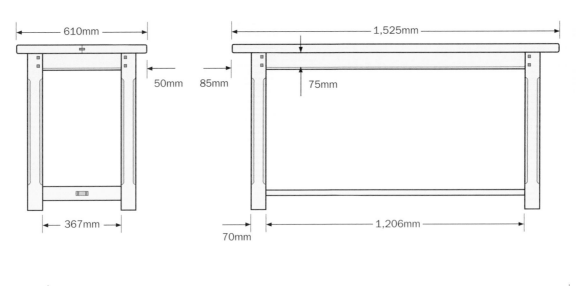

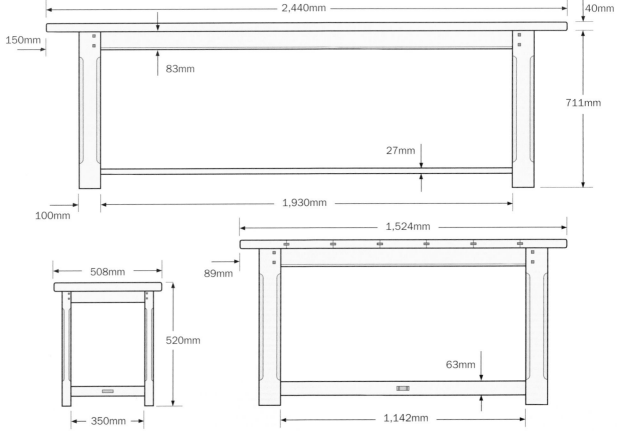

With this step complete, the table could then be dry assembled to achieve the exact measurement of the stretcher rail running down the centre and, on the dining table, the support rail running across the width to help support the top. It also pays to mark out where you want to rout the housings for the buttons to hold down the table tops, and where to stop the chamfers on the legs.

The stretcher rails had through mortice and tenons with walnut wedges for detailing, as well as for construction.

They needed to be clean on the outer edge as this would be visible; so when morticing, try to go though from both sides as this helps prevent splitting out. Alternatively, ensure that you mortice through into a second piece of wood supporting the rail on the morticer. The support rail for the top was a stopped tenon.

With the mortices cut I trim the rails and cut the tenons. Mark out on the tenon the size of the wedge that will look attractive but won't spilt the tenon.

You can then cut out the wedge shape and make the walnut wedges to fit. If you make them slightly tight when the time comes to glue they'll spread slightly to tighten up the joint.

Chamfering the legs

My next step is to chamfer the legs and add the walnut detail to the joints. Traditionally, all the joints were dowel pegged, but for this particular piece the square walnut pegs are there for decoration.

Walnut wedges continue the decorative theme

Lamp table

Lamp table

To complement the dining suite, I made a lamp table. This was much smaller about 508mm (20in) square but carried the same theme and using all the same principles, though on a smaller scale.

The side table construction is the same as its larger companion

Beading on top rails

Tapered mortice

Saw cuts to take wedges

Walnut wedges

Wedged mortice and tenon

After deciding the size, cut the legs out on the morticer; again using the stops if you have that option. Otherwise you'll have to mark them all out. When gluing in the walnut pegs, make them slightly tapered and they'll tighten up and look a lot better when tapping them in with a mallet. Also, whilst working on the legs, chamfer or round off the feet so they don't splinter or chip off on the carpet.

With all the detailing done; the legs and rails sanded and slots routed for the buttons, glue the table up. Here you'll need to add the walnut wedges to the bottom stretcher rail.

The table top

Now for the top – which, due to its sheer size and weight, is the worst part – well, that's what I think.

Machine the boards to the required thickness and, with the table frames made, lay the boards out to get the

desired effect for the top. To join the boards I used 12mm (½in) birch faced ply, grooved to a depth of about 15mm (⅝in) in each board, and spindle straight out the end. This is because the walnut detail is easier to fit when glueing rather than inserting it afterwards. It is vitally important to get the sizes right otherwise the detailing won't look the part. I find it's also easier to glue the table top in stages – I did the two outer boards together and the three middle ones together. After these are glued I took the opportunity to use a speed sander as this saves a lot of cleaning up. Now the three sections can be glued together using the frame to support the top. You'll probably need some friends to help as the top, by now, is very cumbersome – it took four of us to move it!

It's not often you get to clamber around on a dining table; unless, of course, those are the type of parties you

throw. However, the only way I could reach the middle to clean up was to crawl around on the table top!

Before turning the top over, put a 9mm (1½in) bullnose on the edge. Flip the top over and do the same the other side. Before turning it back it pays to apply your chosen finish to limit the amount of times you'll have to turn the top. Obviously the top for the serving table is easier, but all the same operations apply. Apply the finish to the frames and tops; then assemble them using the buttons to fix the tops in place.

PHOTOGRAPHY BY ANTHONY BAILEY

Mark Constanduros
makes a dining room suite –
part two: the chairs

The completed suite

The full monty

In the previous article I went through the design and construction of the various tables – so what is needed now are some chairs to sit on.

A chair is very important to get right: you need to give the body support in the right way. I have always admired the chairs designed by Alan Peters, which allow the timber used for the back splat

> **"A chair is very important to get right: you need to give the body support in the right way"**

to naturally curve and form the support for the sitter's back. I decided to take this idea one step further and upholster the back. The continuing feature from the tables is the walnut (*Juglans sp*) detailing in the joints and so I decided to introduce an additional feature: a bead up the front and back of the chair legs. This bead was also a design detail I could use when it came to making the sideboard.

Tips when making chairs

Before making the real chairs it is always advisable to make a prototype chair, and this is a good opportunity to use odd pieces of timber lying around the workshop. By doing this you can

alter any of the features now rather than later when it may be too late. Having made the prototype I invited the clients to the workshop where they were able to sit in the chair and we could move the padding around until they found a position that suited them.

With the timber and features now decided upon, it was time to start the production... With ten chairs to make you don't want to slip up, so a good idea is to make eleven. In this case, the eleventh chair was made with timber that got rejected for the required ten and so you can also keep it if you don't make any mistakes. Always machine more components than you need because you'll always need an extra one!

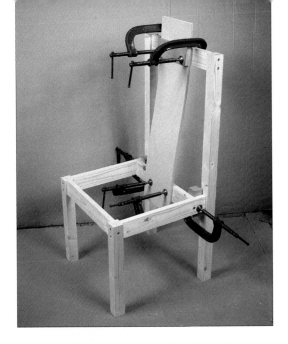

Full size mock-ups are a pre-requisite when chair making

Jig and template in use for shaping the round tops of the legs

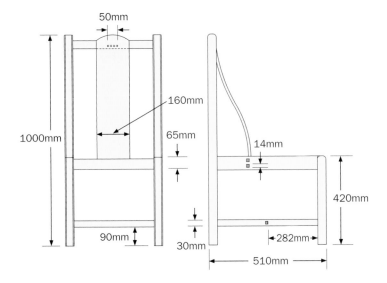

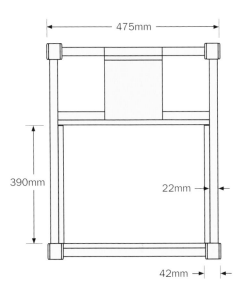

"To make the back splat you'll require the use of the dummy chair"

You can now use the eleventh chair as the guinea pig for all the operations – and believe me you will!

You'll also require a number of jigs which can all be made in MDF: one for the crest rail; one to do the bead around the top of the inside of the front legs, as well as the use of the prototype chair to help create the back splat.

Machining the legs

The first job is to cut out and machine up all the legs. You'll then need to make your first jig: a strip of MDF, say, about 100mm (4in) wide and long enough to support the legs. This jig is required to round the tops of the back legs and round the front part of the top of the front legs. Screw a timber fence to this jig 40mm (1⅝in) from the edge and 80mm (3⅛in) short of the top. At the top of the jig make a nice rounded top that you like, this will be the guide for the bearing or pin to form the shape on the leg.

The shaping was completed on an overhead router. It is possible using a hand router with a bearing guided cutter and a false bed around your work, to help support the router. By doing this before you cut the legs to length means if you get any breakout you can slide the leg up the jig and clean it up.

Beading and trimming

The next task is to run the bead around the edge of the legs. This can be completed on the overhead router, or you can use a router table with a bearing guided 5mm (³⁄₁₆in) beaded edge cutter. The back legs are easy enough but just make sure you have the bead on the front edge running around to the back. The front legs will require a jig in the shape of the top legs, rounded over. As the front edge of the front legs is rounded and the back of them is square, due to the joint, you need the template jig to run the bead in the curve like the back legs. On the inside edge you won't require the jig, as the bead will run right over the top and down the back, but most of it will be removed to allow the seat squab to drop in.

The next job is to trim them all to length ready for morticing. Again, I used the stops on the morticer, marking out all the joints for one chair, then setting the stops up for the others. You could do this with any morticer by cramping ➤

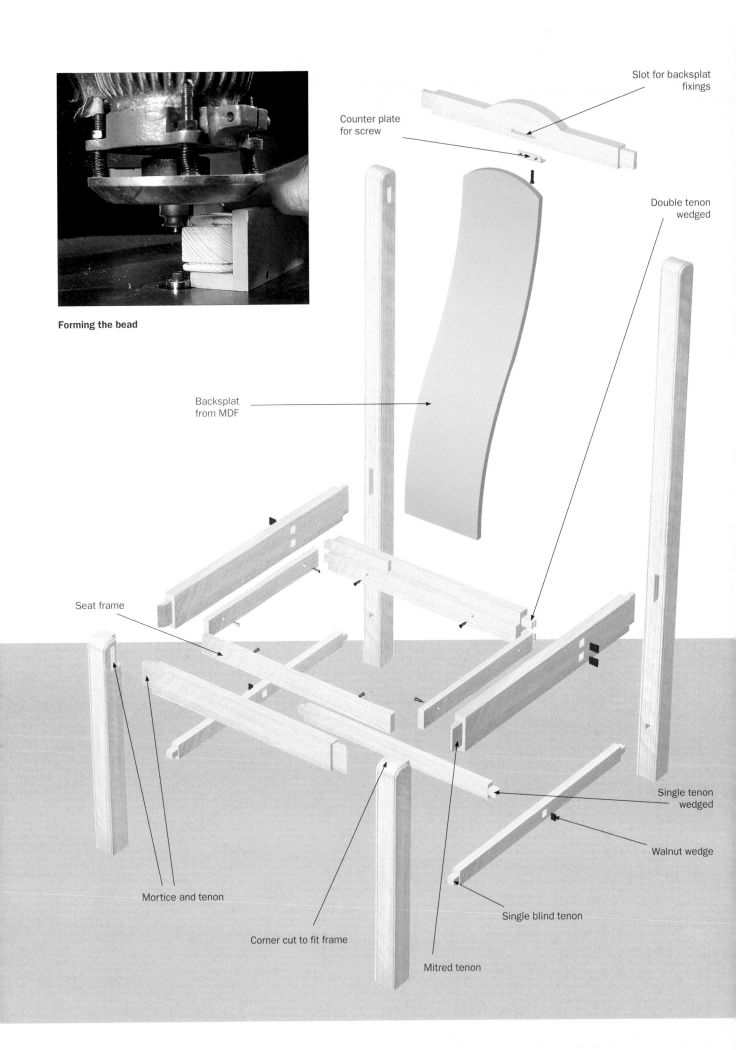

Forming the bead

Slot for backsplat
fixings

Counter plate
for screw

Double tenon
wedged

Backsplat
from MDF

Seat frame

Mortice and tenon

Corner cut to fit frame

Single tenon
wedged

Walnut wedge

Single blind tenon

Mitred tenon

Back splats

To make the back splat you'll require the use of the dummy chair. To get the natural curve, glue together two sheets of 6mm (¼in) MDF in the form of the required curve by cramping it on the back rail and then cramping it to the crest rail, but place a 12mm (½in) packer underneath at the crest rail end. The reason for this is you'll need to let in some of the back splat into the back rail. With the eleventh chair dry cramped you can mark out where the housing will need to go to let in the back splats.

Whilst forming the back splats, carry on cleaning up the chairs and gluing them together. This does take a long time so the break of gluing up the back splats provides a change of scenery! Before you move each splat, mark out the top of the back rail and then you'll know where to position them on the real chairs. When they are all glued up you can cut the splats to width but still leave them over length.

When all the chairs are glued up, position a back splat on the eleventh chair and mark the housing the width of the splat. You'll also require a brass right angle bracket which should be screwed to the back splat and slot into a groove in the bottom of the crest rail. With the housing cut and the groove slotted, place the splat and screw it at the bottom. At the top hold in place and drill through the pre-drilled hole and through the brass. Then put in the screw and this will hold the top in place. When this is upholstered, the upholsterer should fold the padding around the edge of the splat thus filling in the gap between the rail and the splat. With it fixed in place, draw the crest rail shape on the splat and then lose another 5mm (³⁄₁₆in) to allow for the upholstery to fold over the top. Cut out the shape, sand and refit.

The finished bead on the front legs...

... and on the back legs

stops on the back face of the sliding carriage, but you might prefer to mark all the joints out. Then you have to believe in yourself and just go for it! By doing this you'll know that all the joints will correspond – beginning, of course, with the eleventh chair just to make sure it all works.

Machining rails

With all the legs complete, make a start on machining up the seat rails and cresting rail. You'll also need a jig to cut the curve for the crest rail; this governs

"The upholsterer requested an MDF base for these chairs to be covered with fireproof foam and then covered with the customer's requested material"

the shape of the backsplat. To cut the shape of the rail you can use the overhead router or a fluted cuter with a bearing at the top and run the router base on the jig. You can also rout in the slot for the back splat and a screw hole for the fixing. Also fit a brass counter plate for the screw to bed on as this looks better than a worn hole.

Cut to length all the rails, bar the back seating rail as you'll do these last. Then cut all your tenons and make them fit. Remember to do this on the eleventh chair first. With the chair

together in the dry you can square it all up and check the dimension for the back rail. This one is different to the others as it is a double tenon and wedged using walnut.

Divide the tenon up and cut the two small mortices, first starting from the front and then turn over and go through from the back. This will help prevent breakout. With the mortices done you can cut the tenons for the back rail and then carefully cut them to fit. If they are slightly loose, side to side, don't worry as you'll be able to take up any slack using the walnut wedges which will help pull the chair together.

Stretcher rails

The next task is the stretcher rails. Not all chairs have them, but it does look better when they are fitted and they help to hold the chair together at

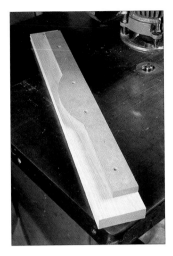

Template for the crest rail

Morticing the legs

Twin stub tenons on the back rail

Forming the back splat for two sheets of 6mm of MDF

the bottom where the legs have a tendency to spread – especially as most people tip their chairs. The centre stretcher rail is also wedged using walnut. Once again, cut the mortice from the back and turn it over to cut through from the front.

The seat

The next step is the seat. In this instance the upholsterer may request what they would like the seat frame to be made of. Traditionally it would be a frame morticed and tenoned together with a horsehair filling. The upholsterer requested an MDF base for these chairs to be covered with fireproof foam and then covered with the customer's requested material.

There are two ways to hold the seat. One is to rebate all the rails and the other is to screw a baton round the

inside of the seat frame. Due to the design of the chair, a baton was required. This helps support the splat in its housing. With all the batons in place, rout out the corners of the front legs if you are brave enough, or else chisel it out using a rounded chisel in the corner. Don't cut it in square as you will weaken the joint.

You can now measure the size of the seat but remember to allow for the thickness of the material and cut your MDF seats. Round the front corners and take the aris of the seat edges so that it doesn't cut into the material.

Conclusion

With the chair all glued up you can give it a final sand and then put on your required finish. I use a 70% satin lacquer finely applied; if it is thick, though, it can look like plastic.

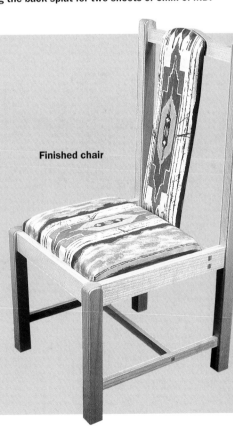

Finished chair

A chip off the old block

The trolley provides flexible and versatile additional workspace

Kevin Ley makes a multi-purpose kitchen trolley

On leaving the RAF in 1987 Kevin Ley set to turning his hobby into a commercial proposition. The former squadron leader designs and makes bespoke furniture from his cottage and workshop in the wilds of Shropshire

PHOTOGRAPHY BY THE AUTHOR
ILLUSTRATIONS BY SIMON RODWAY

When we bought our cottage three years ago my wife thought it perfect – just a few small adjustments were required – one of which turned out to be a complete makeover of the kitchen! Now I understood why it had been so easy to convince her that setting up the workshop was a top priority after we moved in.

The kitchen had fitted units, quite functional but not pretty. The layout and lighting were very poor and the work surfaces badly planned, with insufficient clearance under the top cupboards. A kitchen is, of course, just another workshop so I applied the same basic principles to the overall design.

The first major improvement was to remove the centrally positioned three way spot light cluster – which meant that no matter where you tried to work you would be in your own shadow – and replace it with several low voltage lights, positioned over the areas where light was required. Strip lights were also fitted under the top cupboard bases to light the working surface.

Design

My next step was to provide more usable working surfaces. The main requirement was for a mobile area on which knives could be used to increase flexibility. Hence the basic design of a butcher's block on wheels was born.

It seemed logical to store the knives on board and use the space underneath the top to store a tea tray; an extra cutting board for raw meat; a tiled board to use as a stand for hot items and, on the lower shelf, the bread bin. I felt a 4½ litre supercharged V8 would round it off nicely but was over ruled! The trolley would fit under a standard height worktop but could be moved to any part of the kitchen as required.

Timber selection

The units in the kitchen were standard DIY shed gear in a lovely shade of simulated dark oak – much too sombre for a low ceiling kitchen not over endowed with windows. We decided to redo it in pale sycamore to lighten things up. This timber is a lovely creamy white colour with a uniform, straight grain, a fine, close, even texture and a natural lustre.

I ordered all we required, kiln dried, for the whole kitchen project from Duffields. Having used them for years I know they're careful to end rear the boards to make sure the inevitable marks, from the sticks separating the boards, ▶

Cutting board, tiled hot stand, bread bin

The various trays

The trolley slides neatly away

The double sided raw meat cutting board is made from two pieces of burr, book matched and jointed in the centre, using biscuits and Cascamite with a hardener. A recess is routed in the centre of each face at each end, using a 12mm (½in) core box cutter set to cut 6mm (¼in) deep, thus providing finger grips.

A piece of 19mm (¾in) ply is cut to size and tiled on one side with some spare tiles left over from the kitchen walls. A piece of burr is ten biscuited to each end, with the same finger grip arrangement as the cutting board.

A simple box is made from sycamore as a bread bin. The corners are butted and reinforced with biscuits. A sycamore faced 5mm (³⁄₁₆in) MDF base is glued in to a slot cut in the base. The lid is made from burr and a slot cut in the underside to locate it over the sides. This lid also doubles as a bread board for cutting on.

"A kitchen is, of course, just another workshop so I applied the same basic principles to the overall design"

do not penetrate below the surface. I selected the wood and checked with a small plane just to be sure. To add a little visual detail interest to the sycamore used throughout the kitchen I decided to use burr elm *(Ulmus sp)* pulls on the doors and drawers. I had some big lumps of burr, rescued from a log pile, which had been drying at the back of my timber store for about 12 years. Their time had come, and despite the derision and hilarity of the editorial staff at *F&C*, I decided they would provide a nice, heavy, un-splitable top to the trolley, with the off cuts used for the door and drawer pulls.

Timber preparation

Even though the big irregular chunks of burr had been drying for so long, the moisture content in the middle would still be higher than close to the surface. There were also plenty of faults and blemishes so to get a decent size top, clear of faults, I had to make it up from several pieces. They're cut about 10% over size and stacked with sticks between them in the workshop to let the fibre stresses and moisture content stabilise, before finally making them up.

The sycamore *(Acer pseudoplatanus)* pieces are also cut a bit over size, stacked and sticked in the workshop to condition before starting. Even though this was kiln dried, and had been in my timber store with its dehumidifier for a long period, time was still needed to allow the fibre stresses to stabilise after cutting. Note, the workshop is kept at end use conditions so the conditioning process continues during the making.

Legs and rails

The legs are all cut to size, and the shoulders on the inside edges of the top of the front legs cut on the band saw.

The bulk of the waste for the recesses in the tops of the rear legs is removed with a router and squared off with a chisel. The side edges are stop chamfered on the router table and finished with a scraper, and the bottom edges rounded over to 6mm (¼in).

I had decided to use double biscuit joints to attach the rails to the legs, flush with the outside edge; so the rails are cut to size and the biscuit positions marked. The biscuit slots are also cut at the same time, using only one depth adjustment.

The sides are assembled first, using four number 20 biscuits on the top rail, and two on the bottom, clamped up, measured across the diagonals to ensure it is square, and left to set. The bearer rails for the tray and boards are then screwed to the sides under the top and the sides fitted together by fitting the front and back rails, again with biscuits. Once it was clamped, all the diagonals ➤

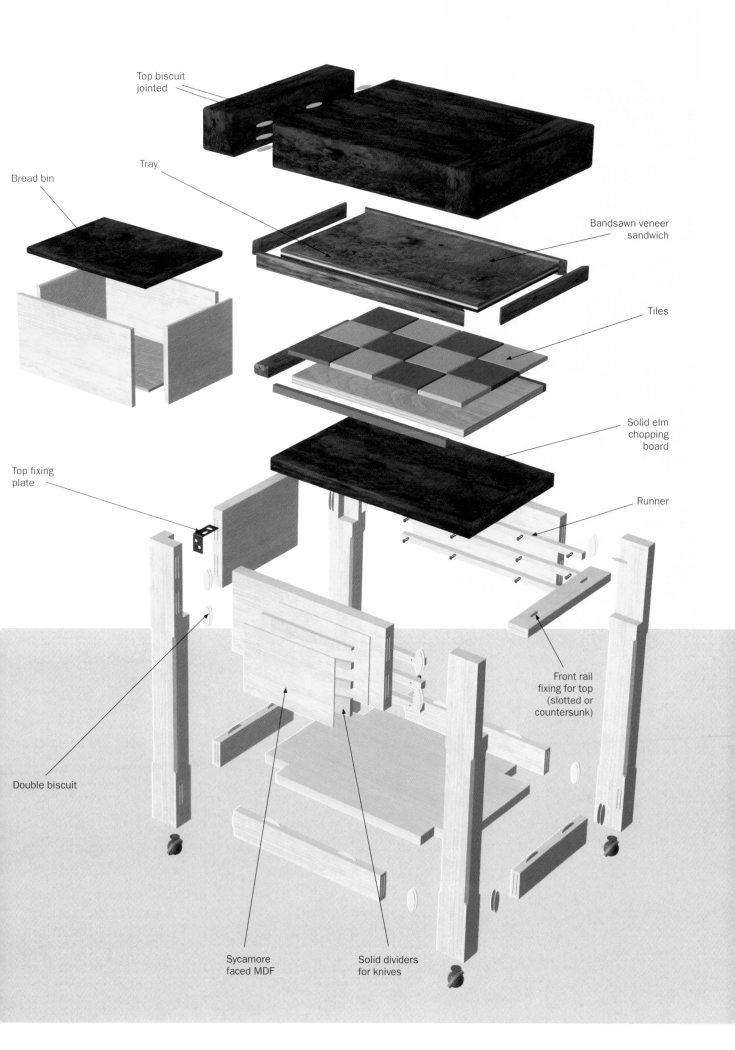

Top biscuit jointed

Tray

Bread bin

Bandsawn veneer sandwich

Tiles

Solid elm chopping board

Top fixing plate

Runner

Double biscuit

Front rail fixing for top (slotted or countersunk)

Sycamore faced MDF

Solid dividers for knives

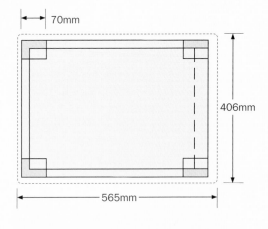

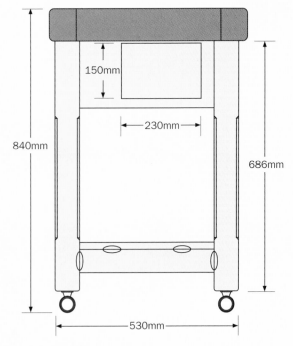

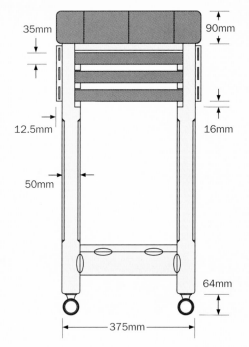

"The floor in the kitchen is riven slate and, therefore, slightly uneven. I managed to find some castors with 'soft' wheels; this considerably improved the ease of movement and reduced noise"

are checked to ensure the whole trolley is square and true, then it's left to cure.

Shelf and knife holders

The bottom shelf is cut to size and the corners – to fit round the legs – cut out on the band saw, then dropped on to the bottom rails and fixed with biscuits.

The knife holders are made up from two pieces of sycamore-faced MDF separated by thin strips of solid sycamore to form the slots for the specific knives. The positions for the

"The trolley has proved to be of enormous general use, giving great flexibility in the kitchen"

strips of wood are marked out around the knives and glued into position using a fast setting PVA glue. The size and spacing of the strips of wood are adjusted so the knife holders on each side are the same size, regardless of the size of the knives they are holding. The knife holders are then glued to the sides of the trolley with Cascamite.

Top

The top is now made up from the six pieces which had been cut from the raw lumps. Burr has such a wild grain it's difficult to assess whether one is gluing end or side grain, and it'll probably change along the join any way! I decided to multi biscuit all the joins and use Cascamite glue with K10 hardener – for its strength and waterproof quality – bearing in mind the top would be washed and oiled regularly. The top is

then fixed to the frame using screws through double counter sunk holes up through the front rail and with expansion plates to the back rail. The plates are fixed to the back rail directly with screws through counter sunk holes, and to the top through the slots. There are two slots at right angles to each other – remembering wood will move across the grain – I made sure to put the screw into the right one. This allowed for the inevitable movement of the top, while holding it flat, and left the clearance required for the underslung tray and boards.

Wheels and tray

The floor in the kitchen is riven slate and, therefore, slightly uneven. I managed to find some castors with 'soft' wheels; this considerably improved the ease of movement and reduced noise.

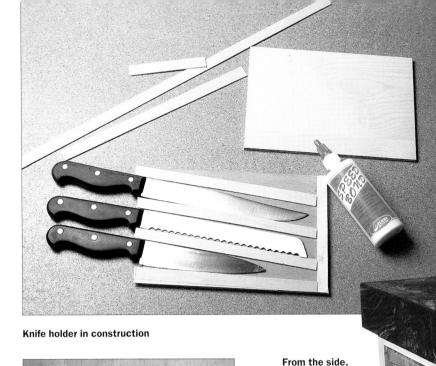

Knife holder in construction

The top is double biscuited all the way round

From the side, showing knife storage

Suppliers

Soft wheel castors:
Archibald Kenrick & Sons
tel: 0121 553 2741
Acrylic finish:
Satin Aqua Cote
mail order from Barfords
tel: 01277 622050

I made the tea tray base by book matching two pieces of 12mm (½in) burr and edge jointing them, not using biscuits. When they were set I made sure both faces were planed flat, and split it in half by deep sawing through the middle on the band saw. The planed side of the resultant, approximate, 6mm (¼in) 'veneers' is glued down to each side of a piece of 5mm (³⁄₁₆in) three-ply, again using Cascamite. It's then placed on the bench, covered with a piece of thick ply and concrete blocks on top, as a makeshift press. When it had cured I put it through the thicknesser a couple of times on each side to reduce the thickness. The tray is completed by putting a simple frame, mitred at the corners, around the base and the base is set in the centre of the frame height to give a double sided tray, with a finger grip at each end to pull the tray out.

Finish and hygiene

All the sycamore is finished with Barfords Aqua Cote, a satin finish, acrylic, water-based, floor varnish. I decided to apply three coats and it is touch dry in 20 minutes but should be left for the full two hour drying time before cutting back between each coat. This finish is extremely tough and helps to prevent the sycamore from yellowing.

The tray and ends of the tiled hot stand are finished with four coats of yacht varnish which protects the surface and allows constant wiping with a damp cloth.

All the cutting boards are finished with olive oil as they would be in contact with food. Oil is a renewable finish and the most suitable for a surface which will be constantly scored. Re-oiling should take place as required.

The wooden cutting boards should, of course, be kept scrupulously clean, for which a kitchen anti-bacterial cleaner is ideal but I use an anti-bacterial spray as well. At least one side of one chopping board should be kept exclusively for raw meat and not used for any other food.

Conclusion

This is a wonderful sandwich-making workstation. One can creep off to a quiet corner and, virtually unnoticed, get on with the important business of making a bacon butty. The trolley has proved to be of enormous general use, giving great flexibility in the kitchen.

Taking the chair

As an ex-architect and photographer, Richard Stevenson trained in furniture design at City of Bristol College before becoming a self-employed designer-maker based in the west of England

PHOTOGRAPHY BY THE AUTHOR
ILLUSTRATIONS BY IAN HALL AND SIMON RODWAY

Richard Stevenson makes
a set of dining chairs

W hen I took the plunge and opened my workshop a couple of years ago, my first commission was a dining table in maple. The clients wanted to sit eight, and occasionally ten, and the design was to be in a robust and unfussy style to serve as a family table for doing homework on as well as entertaining. Although they did not have a mental picture of what they wanted, they said they liked curves.

The result was a rectangular table 2100mm (6ft 8in) long with curved ends and reverse-curved, laminated end rails.

The curved rail on the table also provided the design detail for the chairs

Backing off

Even though I had produced sketches, working drawings, and even a small scale model, the clients had not been able to visualise quite what they were getting and, as this was the first time they had commissioned a piece of

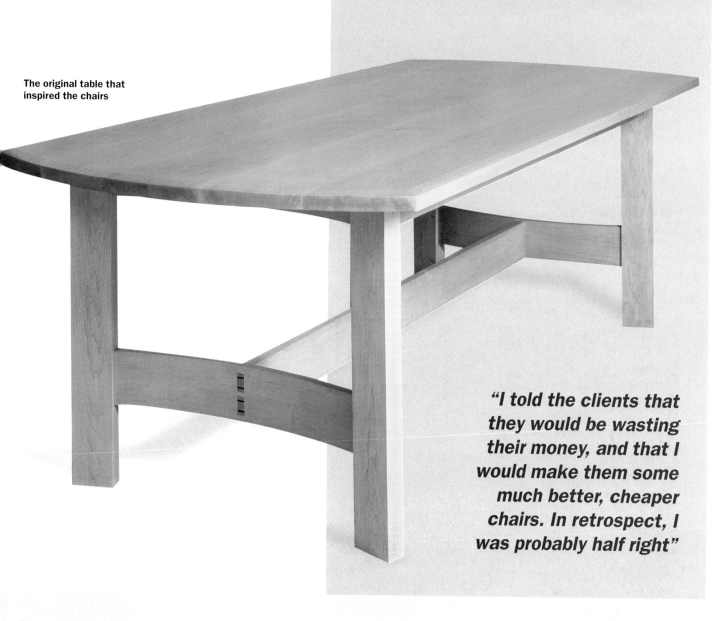

The original table that inspired the chairs

"I told the clients that they would be wasting their money, and that I would make them some much better, cheaper chairs. In retrospect, I was probably half right"

furniture, they had obviously been somewhat apprehensive about the finished piece. Happily it turned out to be just what they wanted, and the subject of suitable chairs was soon raised. Never having made a chair, and being terrified by all the stories I had heard of the complexity of the joinery, not to mention the ergonomics, I suggested that the clients' best course was to look for some ready-made chairs in a suitable style as it would be too expensive to have me make them. This was accepted, I breathed a sigh of relief, and over the next year or so made several other pieces for the same clients.

Bad buy

Early last year I was told that some suitable chairs had been found and, although they were very expensive, the clients thought they were what they wanted, and asked me to have a look at them in the shop. I couldn't believe what I saw. The design was quite acceptable, but the construction was lamentable –

dowelled joints through which daylight could be seen, and steel corner braces with nuts and bolts. Alright for low budget furniture, but eight of these chairs would cost nearly three times as much as my table.

Mis-priced

I told the clients that they would be wasting their money, and that I would make them some much better, cheaper chairs. In retrospect, I was probably half right. The resulting chairs are certainly much better constructed, they are made in maple to match the table, and in my view, are a better design – but I now know why people warned me to beware of such a commission. Although they were much cheaper than the others, they should not have been, with the result that my hourly rate for the job does not bear thinking about.

The pricing of a commissioned piece is the aspect which I seem to have the most difficulty with and, as Paul Richardson has stressed in his column 'Face and

Edge' in *F&C*, it is one which can have a severe effect on one's prosperity.

Happy clients

Anyway, on to the happier side of things – the design and construction of what turned out to be an extremely successful job which delighted my clients, although possibly the altruistic nature of my quotation had a bearing on this.

Design

The design had to be simple and bold to complement the table and, after some doodling, I realised that the curved end sections of the table's frame could be easily adapted to form the chair back frame. This meant more laminating which was done with maple constructional veneers cramped between male and female formers. I debated the merits of purchasing a vacuum bag but, as I had already acquired a morticer for this commission, I could not justify, or afford, the extra expense. One of the problems of a new workshop is that ➤

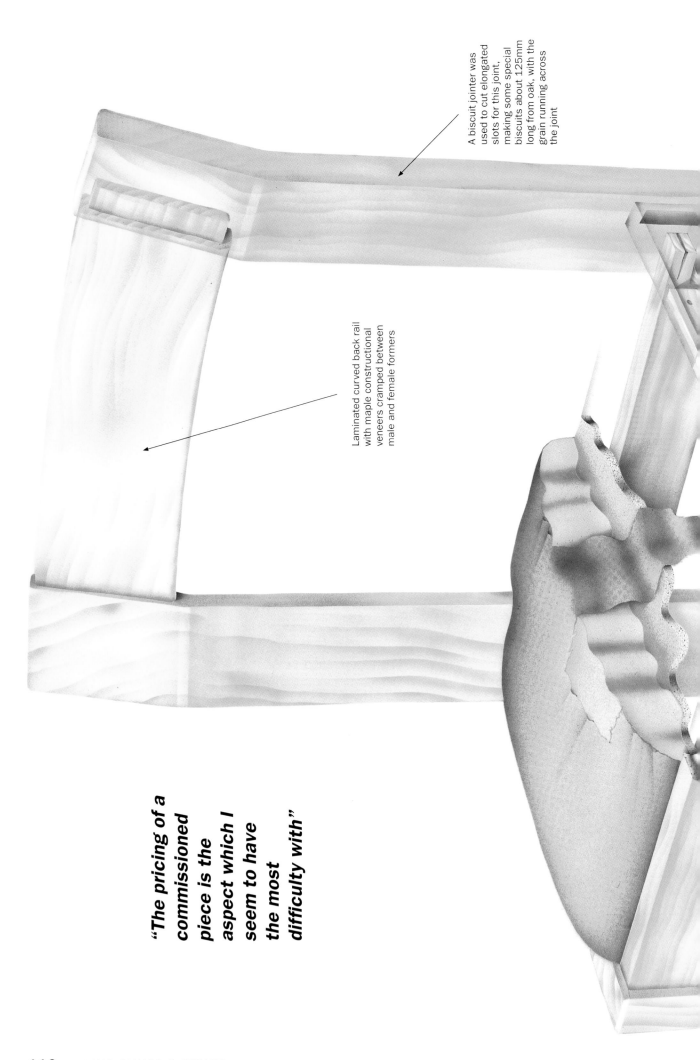

A biscuit jointer was used to cut elongated slots for this joint, making some special biscuits about 125mm long from oak, with the grain running across the joint

Laminated curved back rail with maple constructional veneers cramped between male and female formers

"The pricing of a commissioned piece is the aspect which I seem to have the most difficulty with"

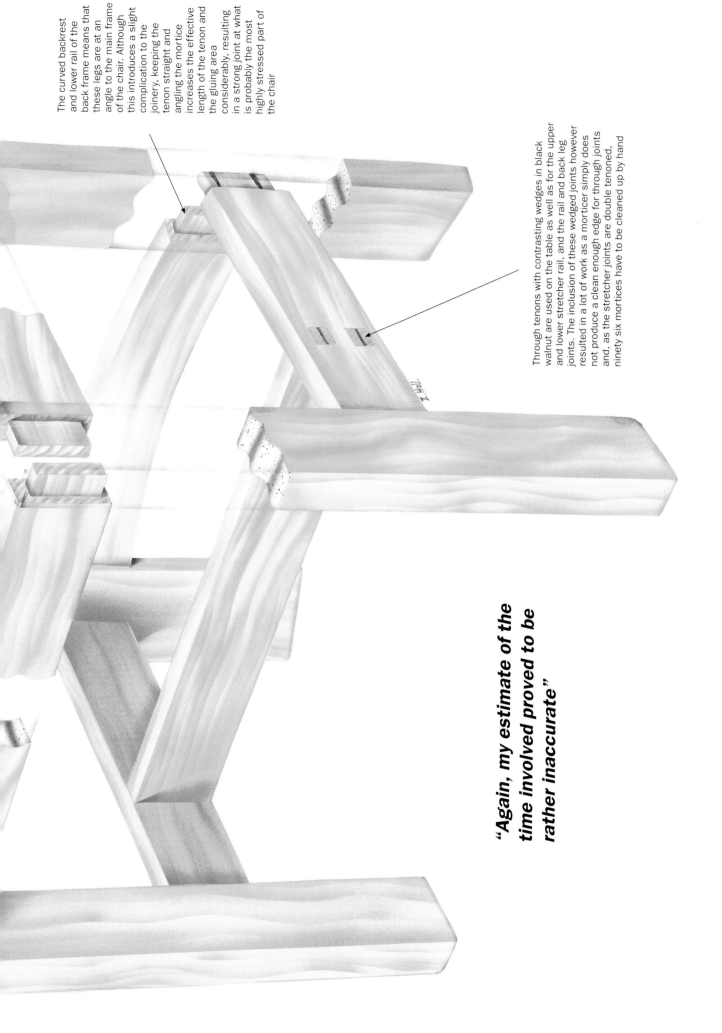

The curved backrest and lower rail of the back frame means that these legs are at an angle to the main frame of the chair. Although this introduces a slight complication to the joinery, keeping the tenon straight and angling the mortice increases the effective length of the tenon and the gluing area considerably, resulting in a strong joint at what is probably the most highly stressed part of the chair

Through tenons with contrasting wedges in black walnut are used on the table as well as for the upper and lower stretcher rail, and the rail and back leg joints. The inclusion of these wedged joints however resulted in a lot of work as a morticer simply does not produce a clean enough edge for through joints and, as the stretcher joints are double tenoned, ninety six mortices have to be cleaned up by hand

"Again, my estimate of the time involved proved to be rather inaccurate"

Detail showing the through-wedged tenons and laminated back rail

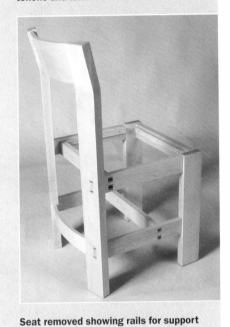

Seat removed showing rails for support

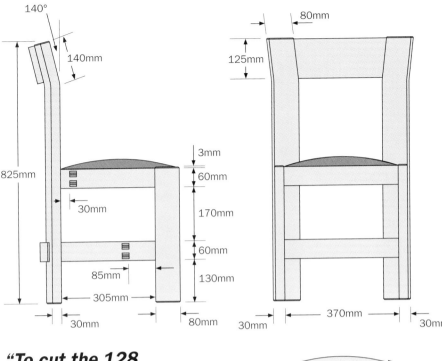

"To cut the 128 wedges to a consistent size I made a simple jig on which strips of walnut were fed through the bandsaw at the necessary angle"

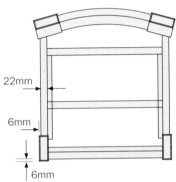

➤ each new job seems to require the purchase of some piece of equipment. Hopefully, at some point such re-investment of previous income will no longer be necessary.

Production line

The table legs were made of a quite heavy rectangular section, and scaling this down for the chair legs resulted in a simple clean design with basic mortice and tenon joinery for all the main framing members. I reasoned that the adoption of a close-as-I-could-manage to a small production line method, and the use of my new morticer, would make the construction efficient in terms of time. Again, my estimate of the time involved proved to be rather inaccurate.

Through tenons

One feature of the table and a sideboard I had made for the same room was through-tenons with contrasting wedges in black walnut and so for the chairs I adopted this for the upper and

lower stretcher/rail, and the rail/back leg joints.

Apart from these, and a simple 3mm (⅛in) chamfer to the tops and bottoms of front and back legs, there is no ornamentation. The inclusion of wedged joints, however, resulted in a lot of work as a morticer simply does not produce a clean enough edge for through joints and, as the stretcher joints were double tenoned, ninety six mortices had to be cleaned up by hand.

Strong joint

The curved backrest and lower rail of the back frame meant that, as is the case with many designs, the legs are at an angle to the main frame of the chair. Although this introduces a slight complication to the joinery, keeping the tenon straight and angling the mortice increases the effective length of the tenon and the gluing area considerably, resulting in a very strong joint at what is probably the most highly-stressed part of any chair, having to withstand

the inevitable after-dinner tilting backwards.

Spindle moulder

The tenons were all cut on a shaper supplied by Axminster Power Tools. Not having any requirement for long runs of mouldings, I bought this machine for use more as a glorified router table than as a small spindle moulder, and in this role it has performed faultlessly. It is extremely satisfying to be able to adjust the fence and the height of the cutter with great precision and, as an added bonus, it is much quieter than a router.

To cut the 128 wedges to a consistent size I made a simple jig on which strips of walnut were fed through the bandsaw at the necessary angle, see Fig 1.

Frame

The frame is finally glued in three parts. Top and bottom rails are assembled with their stretchers and carefully checked for square and wind

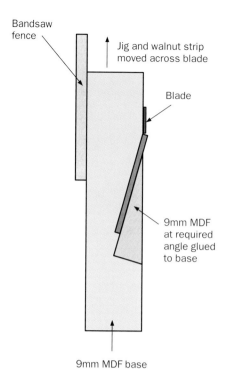

Fig 1 **Bandsaw jig for cutting multiple wedges**

Bandsaw fence

Jig and walnut strip moved across blade

Blade

9mm MDF at required angle glued to base

9mm MDF base

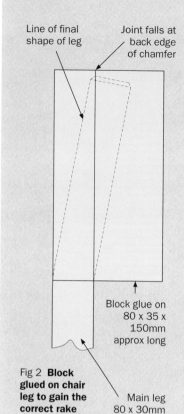

Line of final shape of leg

Joint falls at back edge of chamfer

Block glue on 80 x 35 x 150mm approx long

Fig 2 **Block glued on chair leg to gain the correct rake**

Main leg 80 x 30mm

Rake

To establish the necessary rake to the top of the rear legs for the backrest, I constructed a full scale mock-up in pine and was lucky to get it right at my second attempt. In this case it turned out to be 14°.

I could have bandsawn the legs from sections 75mm (3in) thick, but I felt this would have been very wasteful. I could also, I suppose, have tried steam bending, but this was more uncharted water, and I think 30mm (1¼in) thick maple would have been quite a challenge. I eventually settled on gluing a block of maple about 175mm (6⅞in) long and 40mm (1⅝in) thick to the top back of each leg. The profile was then drawn on to the edge using an MDF template, the shape cut as accurately as possible on the bandsaw and finished off with a drum sander, planes and scrapers. Provided that care is taken to make the joint fall at the back of the chamfer to the top of the leg, this results in an economical solution with no visible change in grain direction. I tested this theory by making a second chair in pine, this time complete with correct joinery. This proved to be time well spent, as not only can the design be fine-tuned, but cramping arrangements can be worked out. Perhaps more importantly, the client's final approval of the design can be obtained before cutting the real stuff. You also end up with a useful workshop chair.

Chamfered top of legs

before being glued. Front and back legs and rails are similarly separately glued, and the final stage is to assemble the three sections. The most tricky part of the operation is the accurate fitting of the backrest to the rear legs, as the rake introduces compound angles, and fine-tuning with a well-sharpened block plane is necessary.

I used a biscuit jointer to cut elongated slots for this joint, and made some special biscuits about 125mm long from oak, with the grain running across the joint. The lower curved rail is dowelled to the legs, as it is not wide enough to biscuit. This member, whilst contributing to the overall strength is actually more important as a visual element in the link with the table design.

Front legs

The front legs, instead of the more orthodox square section, are of the same elongated rectangular form as the back pair (80 by 30mm) but set in a different plane, and this, as well as allowing a long tenon at the rails, gives a very pleasing degree of asymmetry in the chair's elevations, the proportions seeming to change depending on the angle of view.

The finished chair seems to me to be almost childlike or primitive in its form which perhaps says something about my approach to design – I think it is important to introduce elements into a design to stimulate the eye, and it is not necessary to go for bizarre shapes to achieve this.

Completed construction

The construction is completed by the addition of an upholstered base of 9mm MDF which is carried on the back stretcher, and maple bearers which are fixed with brass screws to the front and top rails. As this stretcher is inset from the back legs, from the back, the seat appears to have no support which introduces another element of tension to the design.

Finish

The chairs are finished with Danish oil, well rubbed down with fine steel wool and when the complete set was placed around the table, the clients were very pleased, and I felt that the time taken to complete the commission had been well spent, even though it had considerably exceeded my estimate. The experience also was very valuable in itself, as I am now able to undertake future commissions for chairs with much less apprehension.

Selby-based Ian Lyons spent 35 years in engineering before taking early retirement and enrolling as a mature student on a BTEC Furniture Making and Restoration course at Leeds College of Art and Design.

PHOTOGRAPHY BY THE AUTHOR
MAIN ILLUSTRATION BY IAN HALL
ADDITIONAL BY SIMON RODWAY

Ian Lyons makes a ladies' dressing table inspired by Gillow's of Lancaster

Gillow's pieces are synonymous with craftsmanship, elegance and proportion

All dressed up

I first came into contact with Gillow's of Lancaster furniture at Keswick museum in the Lake District. I liked the proportion, elegance and exceptional craftsmanship.

During my BTEC National Diploma course, and through educational visits, I had more exposure to Gillow's work and decided to base my major project upon their Regency period. It was important the piece fitted the intended room setting and had more storage space than the single layer usual to this period. It was also important the design maintained neo-classical proportions.

Design

Designing the piece was aided by the use of Autocad – a skill I learnt at college – which is an excellent tool for drawing development.

The dressing table only became 'knock down' when I had problems machining the six long legs; my solution was to return to my engineering roots. The reeded portion of the legs could be reduced to manageable proportions and a threaded bar could be tapped into the sleeved leg, secured with epoxy resin and, finally, a 3mm (1/8in) steel through pin. Using this idea meant all the leg parts had to be made with engineering precision. The test of this accuracy is when all parts come together for an end of year exhibition!

Leg construction

To maintain the leg and corner-block grain pattern and colour, the two corner-blocks and leg are cut from the same blank and hard stamped to ensure correct positioning on the lathe. This is repeated for the remaining five blanks. The six lower leg blanks ends are squared and centred for turning, taking care not to remove the identifying stamps. One leg is sample turned to gain knowledge of the process; also to act as a template for the copy lathe. The six lower leg blanks are machined using the copy lathe, cleaned and detailed by hand. These lower legs are then transferred to the overhead router so 12 reeds could be cut down the leg. This is difficult as the variation in grain patterns didn't give constant cutting characteristics. The reeding is then cleaned up using a scraper shaped to the reed profile.

The legs are sanded and marked for centre; drilled by 8mm (5/16in) and tapped in a 10mm (3/8in) coarse thread to a depth of 30mm (1 1/8in). A threaded bar is introduced with a layer of epoxy resin to bond the thread, an outer sleeve of brass is also fitted to improve the strength. When the assembly is dry a steel dowel, 3mm (1/8in) diameter is drilled through the lower leg boss to secure the whole assembly.

The legs are then given two coats of shellac sanding sealer, rubbed down between each coat and finally 'bodied up' with garnet polish.

Carcass construction

The cherry (*Prunus sp*) is examined

**Above: Leg rods and spacers
Below: Zebrano cross-banded sub-frame in place**

"All the internals of the drawers are sanded to remove any marks and dry assembled to check for accuracy"

Cross banding and reeding

A line, parallel to the edge, is marked at 40mm (1⁵/₈in) to take the cherry (*Prunus sp*) cross banding, a knife line is scored and any excess veneer and glue is removed, with a sharp chisel, to the MDF. Suitable cherry veneer is cut to 45mm (1³/₄in) width with the grain running across the band, taking care to match the spacing between yearly growth lines as near as possible. These are cut and fitted to each edge with veneer tape ties allowing the veneer to be folded back to apply adhesive. The top is pressed for seven minutes again.

Fortunately all veneers glued perfectly, just leaving the rounded corner sections; each corner filled with three by 30° veneers with the grain running radially so the cross banding grain matches round the corners. These are applied with PVA and clamped with a small G-clamp and MDF block until adhered. All the veneer tape is dampened and removed, and positions marked for stringing. A straight edge is clamped to the top at 36mm (1³/₈in) and 42mm (1¹¹/₁₆in) centres to cut the stringing line grooves which are produced using a small hand router and 1.5mm (¹/₁₆in) cutter, to a depth of 1mm (³/₆₄in). All edges are cleaned up and the boxwood (*Buxus sempervirens*) stringing cut, mitred and fitted using PVA adhesive which is slightly watered down. When the PVA is fully dried, the stringing is dressed with a sharp paring chisel and sanded down to the level of the veneered surface.

The edge moulding is cut using a scratch stock to give a reeded edge, historically correct for the piece. I manufactured the scratch stock using a shaped hardwood block and a blade ground and filed to shape.

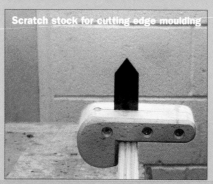

Scratch stock for cutting edge moulding

A cutting gauge is used to remove the waste for the cross banding

in the sawn state; the wildest grain being reserved for the six drawer fronts and four side sections. The two back sections and four inner partitions are ripped down from the remaining wood – which included a little sapwood – and finished to size.

The mortice and tenons are marked and machined at the same time to maintain consistency. All faces and edges are sanded to a finish, as it is not possible to sand when fully assembled. The shoulder lengths and joint fit are checked on all components followed by a dry assembly using clamps. When satisfied, Cascamite glue is mixed and the components assembled and clamped – the leg spacers are inserted and through bolts are fitted to maintain alignment. Each dimension is checked, as is the squareness of all components. Excess glue is removed with a damp cloth and the whole assembly put safely to one side for 24 hours to dry. The drawer runners' guides and kickers are drilled for countersunk screws and

fitted with a dummy block to ensure all parts are accurately positioned. The runners and stretchers are dimensioned from the carcass, jointed and fitted.

Table top

Using the panel saw, an MDF sheet is cut to the appropriate size. When resizing, it's imperative here to use the extraction system and wear a dust mask.

The centre break section is then cut using the bandsaw and trued using a bull nosed plane and hand chisels. Sizing allowance is made for lippings to be glued to all edges. Suitable lengths of sawn cherry are edge planed and ripped to 24mm (¹⁵/₁₆in) square thicknessed to 20mm (²⁵/₃₂in) square. Mitre angles are cut and all components fitted together before gluing. The lipping is marked in position and individually fitted.

PVA glue is applied to the lippings and these are positioned using masking tape. The glue cured using a RF bonding machine. The long sections are

glued first, and any excess glue removed from the mitred surfaces; the process repeated until all edges are completed. After twenty minutes or so, a sharp plane is used to take the lippings down to the MDF, which is then passed through the wide belt sander until all edges are level and smooth.

Sufficient veneer is selected to veneer the whole top and bottom. I use beech (*Fagus sp*) as a backing sheet, the eucalyptus (*Myrthceae sp*) is book matched and edged to give a clean joint line and positioned to the top. In preparation, the veneer press is cleaned of all debris using cleaning solution and then a release agent is spread equally over all the surfaces. The press is closed with heat on both sides to dry the release agent and, when dry, the top plate is selected for heat only. The MDF is wiped down with a damp cloth to remove any dust and pre-condition the board. The PVA adhesive is spread equally, one side at a time, positioned and put through the press for seven ▶

Sub-frame

The sub-frame is placed upon the bottom section of the dressing table, centralised and the holes marked through, thus giving a centre to mark the cut out for the six detail spacers. These are cut out using a bandsaw and shaped with a sanding drum to the correct profile. The whole outer surface is then cross banded in zebrano (*Microberlinia brazzavillensis*) veneer, sanded to 240 grit with the grain. Two coats of sanding sealer are applied and finally polished with pale French polish.

Table top

Sufficient veneer is selected to veneer the whole top and bottom. I use beech (*Fagus sp*) as a backing sheet, the eucalyptus (*Myrthceae sp*) is book matched and edged to give a clean joint line and positioned to the top. In preparation, the veneer press is cleaned of all debris using cleaning solution and then a release agent is spread equally over all the surfaces. The press is closed with heat on both sides to dry the release agent and, when dry, the top plate is selected for heat only. The MDF is wiped down with a damp cloth to remove any dust and pre-condition the board. The PVA adhesive is spread equally, one side at a time, positioned and put through the press for seven minutes; this process is then repeated for both sides, checking for cleanliness on each insertion. All veneering is cleaned up and the adhesion checked, any defects being corrected. Great care is needed to be taken when removing excess veneer.

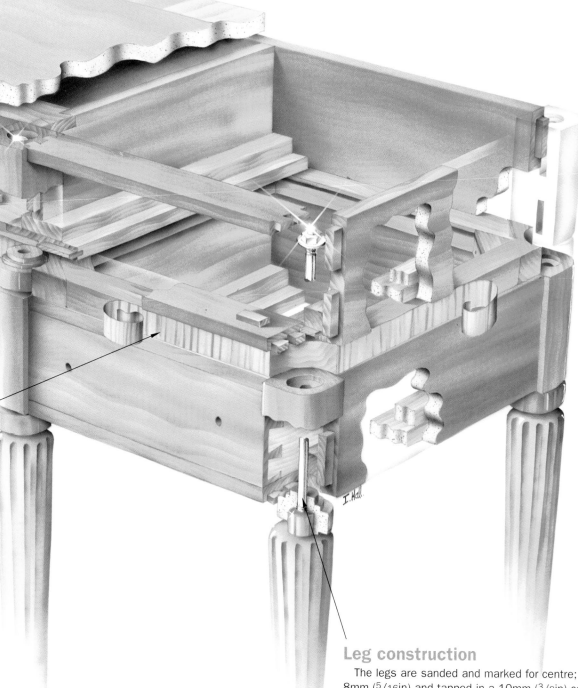

Leg construction

The legs are sanded and marked for centre; drilled by 8mm ($5/16$in) and tapped in a 10mm ($3/8$in) coarse thread to a depth of 30mm ($1^1/8$in). A threaded bar is introduced with a layer of epoxy resin to bond the thread, an outer sleeve of brass is also fitted to improve the strength. When the assembly is dry a steel dowel, 3mm ($1/8$in) diameter is drilled through the lower leg boss to secure the whole assembly.

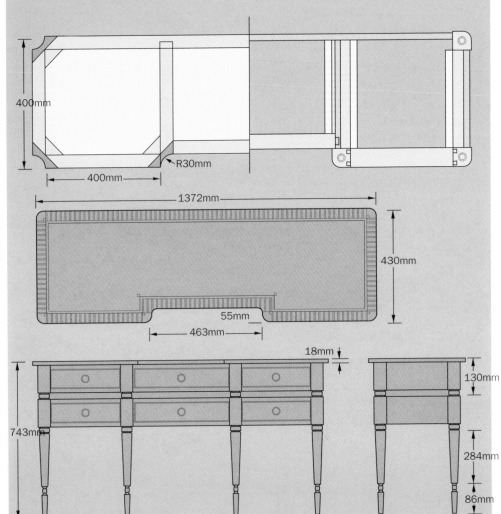

400mm

R30mm

400mm

1372mm

430mm

55mm

463mm

18mm

743mm

130mm

284mm

86mm

Top carcass in position on rods

"I first came into contact with Gillow's of Lancaster furniture at Keswick museum in the Lake District. I liked the proportion, elegance and exceptional craftsmanship"

> minutes; this process is then repeated for both sides, checking for cleanliness on each insertion. All veneering is cleaned up and the adhesion checked, any defects being corrected. Great care is needed to be taken when removing excess veneer.

Sub-frame

Tulipwood (*Dalbergia sp*) is ripped down and thicknessed to a finished size of 32 by 40mm (1¹/4 by 1⁵/8in).The sections are cut to length the ends squared and assembled using a biscuit jointer. The corner sections are cut on the diagonal to increase the strength in that area, to allow for the semi-circle removal, then backed up with corner fillets cut from tulipwood and glued into place. When dry, the whole assembly is thicknessed through the wide band sander to finish dimension of 30mm (1¹/8in).

Rebates are cut for dust boards around each internal section to a depth of 7mm (⁹/32in) and dust boards are cut from 6mm ply; there is potential

here for secret drawers.

The sub-frame is then placed upon the bottom section of the dressing table, centralised and the holes marked through, thus giving a centre to mark the cut out for the six detail spacers. These are cut out using a bandsaw and shaped with a sanding drum to the correct profile. The whole outer surface is then cross banded in zebrano (*Microberlinia brazzavillensis*) veneer, sanded to 240 grit with the grain. Two coats of sanding sealer are applied and finally polished with pale French polish.

Detail spacers

Sufficient mahogany (*Khaya sp*) is cut using the bandsaw, and finished to 55mm (2¹/4in) square, centred and each section turned to the required dimension. One modification occurred when the rounded centre section revealed too much of the underlying framework, so the design had to be altered to a squared off profile. These spacers provide the location between

the top and bottom carcass, so care must be taken in the sizing. The spacers are then sanded, sealed and finished in the same polish.

Drawer construction

The wildest grain cherry and tulipwood is ripped down and thicknessed to size. The drawer front ends are squared off and hand fitted to each position. This sets the width of the drawer to the carcass and the drawer back is cut to the same length. The drawer sides are cut to length – squared on a shooting block. Then, using a cutting gauge, all the pins are marked for the dovetails, each piece of wood being identified to its relevant position by laying the four drawer components end to end and marking the adjoining corners with a semi circle and numbers one to four. There is a 4mm (⁵/32in) groove round the inside of each drawer to take the drawer bottom; this necessitates the dovetails' positioning so the housing would not show through and be hidden by the

Right-hand view showing drawer detail

Cross banding, stringing lines and top edge reeding

A tube spanner is used to secure
the legs to the frames

Rear detail

dovetails. I used lapped dovetails to the front and through dovetails at the rear.

When a satisfactory fit is achieved, the spindle moulder is set up to cut the 4mm (5/32in) housing for the drawer bottoms. The position of the groove is marked on each piece of wood so there would be no confusion during cutting.

All the internals of the drawers are sanded to remove any marks and dry assembled to check for accuracy. The six drawer components are separated and marked to prevent confusion. The bottoms are then measured from the housings and cut on the panel saw from 4mm (5/32in) birch ply sheet, cleaned up with a block plane and checked for square. Each drawer is assembled using Cascamite glue and sash clamps, spacers are required to clear the protruding pin ends. Make diagonal checks for squareness before leaving to dry.

The spindle moulder is used to cut the rebate for the 3mm (1/8in) cherry cockbeading which is fitted full width

on the top of the drawer, ie 20mm (25/32in) wide with a 3mm (1/8in) over-hang, and to the depth of the pins on the bottom and sides, all corners are mitred.

Assembly

The sub-frame is laid into place on the top of the bottom carcass, six leg spacers fitted and centralised. Using G-clamps to maintain position, three 10mm (3/8in) dowel holes are drilled through the spacer into the sides and back, and the dowels fitted. The top carcass is then located onto the spacers and checked for gaps – no adjustment is necessary. The six legs can then be located into their correct positions using a large washer, to spread the weight; the nut being tightened in the recess using a 10mm (3/8in) ring span-ner. The top is centralised and fitted with expansion plates.

Finish

The whole assembly is sanded down, finishing in 240 grit. All surfaces are

given a coat of sanding sealer, the top had two coats to seal and fill. When dry, all surfaces are rubbed down to 240 grit.

Using a rubber and garnet polish, all exterior surfaces are bodied up to be later de-nibbed and finally french polished. The drawers are checked for fit and period pull rings fitted.

Conclusion

I was pleased with the overall effect, and the colour improves as the months go by. The original length was taken from an existing piece of furniture to fit neatly into an alcove. I had to modi-fy this, during the construction stage, to allow the legs to clear the skirting boards. In retrospect, the drawer sides should have been made from oak (*Quercus sp*) as I have had problems since, with the drawers sticking due, I believe, to using tulipwood which seems to be particularly susceptible to climatic change. The design allows two bedside tables to be made from the outside drawer units.

INDEX